THE SPORTSMAN'S GUIDE TO SWAMP CAMPING

THE SPORTSMAN'S GUIDE TO SWAMP CAMPING

For Your Fuller Enjoyment of
Fishing, Hunting, Backpacking
Canoeing, and Boating

J. Wayne Fears

David McKay Company, Inc.

NEW YORK

The author and publisher are deeply grateful to the editor and publisher of *Southern Outdoors* magazine for permission to reprint from articles by J. Wayne Fears that have appeared there.

Library of Congress Cataloging in Publication Data

Fears, J   Wayne, 1938–
The sportsman's guide to swamp camping.

Includes index.
1. Swamp camping. 2. Swamp camping—United States.   I. Title.
GV198.95.F4   796.5′4   79-15732
ISBN 0-679-51354-X

1 2 3 4 5 6 7 8 9 10
Manufactured in the United States of America

This book is dedicated to my parents—my dad gave me an appreciation of wild places and taught me the skills to live there, and my mom gave me the appreciation of the written word and the skills to put the outdoors on paper.

CONTENTS

THE SPORTSMAN'S GUIDE
TO SWAMP CAMPING

1

Why Camp in a Swamp?

The word swamp means many things to many people. To some it means a wet, forbidding environment not fit for human habitation. To others it means a place rich in game and fish, where camping is an adventure and where peace of mind comes easy.

The dictionary states that a swamp is a lowland region saturated with water. In 1976 the U.S. Department of the Interior's Fish and Wildlife Service came up with their official definition: "Swamp is all wetlands with greater than 50 percent of the area in cover of woody plants; that is, trees and brush, vines, etc."

Many sportsmen confuse marshes with swamps. The marsh is almost totally void of any bushes or trees. Most marshes are created by tidal activity and are usually in an area with high saline or alkaline content in the soil. Marshes are usually covered in grasslike plants.

Other people mistake bogs for swamps. Bogs are usually the remains of ancient lakes. Swamps have a covering of trees and woody plants, but bogs are covered with mosses, ferns, and lichens. Until you step in a bog, you usually don't see the water. Then the bog becomes like a wet sponge.

As we study swamps, we learn that their origins are varied. Many are the results of centuries of change in river flows. Swamps along the Mississippi River were formed this way. Some swamps are the result of glacial activity. Swamps around the Great Lakes are of this type. Still other swamps were created by falling meteorites (the Carolina Bays, for instance) and by receding oceans (the Okefenokee Swamp). Today, new swamps are being created by the activity of beavers. There seem to be almost as many ways that swamps were created as there are swamps. The important thing is that we have swamps and that there are swamps in almost every area of North America.

When you as a sportsman begin to seriously consider doing your hunting, fishing, camping, canoeing or boating in the swamps, you may be surprised at how much negative talk you will hear about swamps in general. For centuries, American sportsmen have been kept out of game-rich swamps by horror tales and folklore. The terms snake, beast, quicksand, black panther, poisonous spiders, lost, alligators, and so on have all been overused when associated with swamps. Movies and television have capitalized on these fears by playing up to them in hundreds of misleading movies filmed in a swamp setting.

Historians tell us that this false fear of swamps came about during the early exploration of North America. Since there are few swamps in Europe, the European explorers avoided swamps. Lack of experience with such places made the explorers consider them mysterious. The Indians, recognizing the white man's fear of swamps, told him frightening stories to keep the swamps to themselves. With the passing of each generation the swamp stories grew and were handed down as fact. We still have false swamp fears with us today.

Not everyone, however, has seen our swamps as fearsome places. Some people have seen them as places of hidden wealth—the kind you can put in the bank. Many of the swamps have been the targets of development. Today people live, farm, and work on land that was once a wild and free swamp. Other swamps have been almost fatal victims of drainage attempts. As I write this book, many of our fish-and-game-rich swamps are in danger as the heavy hand of "progress" pushes deeper into wild places.

Swamps are among our last wilderness areas. Because of the fear and ignorance so many people have of them, there are still a good number of swamps scattered over North America that remain in their wild state. These swamps are the last "hideouts" for many of our endangered plants and animals. They are also great water-storage areas and are constantly recharging underground water supplies. The trees and lush plant life in these swamps are helping to keep us in oxygen. Many of the swamp streams are purifying water as it slowly meanders through the swamp.

Perhaps of equal importance is the swamp's overlooked role of providing recreation and adventure for the sportsman and his family. Swamps are excellent game-and-fish habitats, and nowhere will the sportsman find better hunting and fishing. Because swamps are rich in suitable wildlife habitat and have suffered less from the pressures of progress than any other part of the American landscape, they constitute the last sportsman's paradise.

Slowly but surely, the modern-day sportsman is learning what the Cajuns of Louisiana have known for generations—"There ain't nothing to fear in the swamp. Learn to live in her and she will treat you right."

In this book, I mean to show you how you can go into the swamp and live in comfort. The extra dimension of camping, added to your hunting and fishing skills, will turn your swamp travel into an adventure. To defy the fears and mystiques of the swamp and to live for days at a time in it has been a challenge of sportsmen since the early days of the Seminole Indians.

I shall never forget a day many years ago when, as a teenager, I was putting my camping and trapping gear into my wooden boat, preparing for a week of swamp trapping. Several tourists had stopped at a nearby store

The extra dimension of camping, when added to your fishing or hunting skills, will turn your swamp travel into an adventure.

for gas. Seeing me at the boat dock, on a waterway that led into a swamp, they came over out of curiosity and stared. They could not believe I was actually going to camp in that "nasty" swamp. Little did they know that I had not been able to sleep nights before the departure date because I was so excited over going into that beautiful swamp. As I shoved the boat off and started paddling, I heard one of them say, "He is *cra-zy.* I wouldn't go into that jungle for all the gold in Fort Knox." At that moment, I felt 10 feet tall.

Deer hunters, squirrel hunters, moose hunters, duck hunters, bass anglers, bluegill anglers, trout anglers, and scores of other sportsmen have, for years, lost precious time getting into a swamp early in the morning and getting out at night to reach some distant motel or campground to avoid a night in the swamp. Had they camped in the swamp, their sport would have been at their doorstep and their trip would have been a much more memorable adventure.

As we explore swamp camping together in this book, you will see just how simple it really is. Camping is camping regardless of where you are, and the basics are somewhat the same. The chief difference in swamp camping is that your wet environment will require an alteration, sometimes great sometimes small, in your travel skills, your camping techniques, and your awareness of new surroundings.

Early in my outdoor career, I was privileged to spend 2 exciting years exploring swamps with the late Richard Darlington of Quitman, Georgia, an expert in the then unknown field of swamp living. Richard was a living example of how swamp camping takes average camping skills one step further and hones them into an art. He was an artist in outdoor living, and it always amazed me how fast he could convert a small dry spot of land

These sportsmen are stopping for lunch in the Alapaha River Swamp. By camping they'll eliminate time and expense of daily trips to and from motel. Credit: Georgia Industry & Trade.

between two cypress trees into a comfortable camp. It made little difference whether the time was a hot, mosquito-infested July night or a bone-chilling January morning. "Show me a person who is an experienced swamp camper," he used to tell Boy Scout groups who studied swamp camping under his leadership, "and I will show you a master outdoorsman."

With Richard's statement in mind, let's see how you too can become a swamp camper.

2

Swamp-Camping Equipment

The selection of swamp-camping equipment should be made with the same forethought you would give to selecting gear for a mountain-climbing expedition or a desert-crossing trip. The swamp is a special environment that requires somewhat special equipment. I don't mean to imply that the equipment must be expensive. It need not be. But it must be equipment that will ensure your comfort and safety.

A good example of how simple good swamp-camping equipment can be is the gear used by the swamp fishermen in south Georgia. Soon after I graduated from college, I moved to south Georgia to lead an experimental wildlife-management program. The swamps along the Withlacoochee River fascinated me, and soon I met a group of fishermen who spent most of their free time camping and fishing along the river.

These men were expert swamp campers, and they chose gear that would enable them to avoid wetness and be protected from insects. The equipment was also selected for compactness because these fishermen always went into the swamps in a narrow 12-foot-long homemade wooden boat pushed by a 3- or 4-horsepower outboard motor. There simply wasn't room for a lot of gear.

Each man's personal gear consisted of a jungle hammock, wool blanket, knife, and waterproof matches. This simple gear was stuffed into a metal lard bucket, which had a tight-fitting lid. That, along with his fishing tackle, was all the equipment he carried.

One boat always carried a large Dutch oven, a cloth sack of cooking utensils, a plastic container of cooking oil, corn meal, a side of bacon, a case of beer, and one kerosene lantern. These fishermen lived off fish, hush puppies, and bacon.

To the novice, this sounds like a crude form of living, but it was far from it. I spent many enjoyable weekends in the swamps with these sportsmen, and I was never uncomfortable. They had the right equipment for the Withlacoochee River Swamp, and they were masters at using it.

Though I don't recommend that all swamp campers go as light as my Georgia friends, I do suggest that common sense and knowledge be applied to selecting equipment. Swamps in different parts of the country occasionally present somewhat different problems to campers, but as far as equipment is concerned, what will work well in Michigan in the summer will work just as well in Florida. The chief differences in swamp-camping equipment are between what's used in summer camping and what's used in winter camping, but this is also true of camping outside of swamps.

In order to discuss swamp-camping equipment, let's think of your swamp camp as a small home: it has a bedroom, a kitchen, and a bathroom. Work out sensible equipment to fit these needs and you're well on your way to fun living in the swamp.

THE SWAMP BEDROOM

More camping trips are spoiled by poor sleeping conditions than by any other cause I know. The fishing or hunting can be slow, the weather wet, and the food just so-so. As long as you can get a good night's sleep, you can put up with it and even enjoy it. But throw in uncomfortable sleeping conditions and you're ready to pack up and go home.

Shelter—The first step toward a good night's sleep is to have shelter suited to the conditions of your camping environment. Many so-called swamp campers boast of sleeping in swamps in brush lean-tos or in the bottom of a canoe. I have done both, but it was out of necessity. I don't recommend either practice for sportsmen who are in the swamp for recreation.

During the summer, a lean-to can be the place with the most mosquitoes. You are low to the damp ground. If you don't have netting, the flying pests will feast on you. Sleeping in a canoe used to be necessary in the Okefenokee Swamp before the U.S. Fish and Wildlife Service built camping platforms along the trails. I have spent many nights sleeping in my canoe in the swamp, but I can't recall any of them being comfortable. In fact, I can remember one night when an electrical storm dumped several inches of rain on me. The result was like trying to sleep in a bathtub with the drain closed and the water running.

Several shelters do an excellent job in the swamp. One is the jungle hammock. No one seems to know where the jungle hammock was developed, but it first came to the attention of swamp campers during World War II through its use by our armed forces in the South Pacific. This versatile hammock has a bottom of heavy canvas, sides made of mosquito-proof netting, and a top designed for protection from rain. They can be bought in army-navy stores. The jungle hammock is ideal for use when you camp in areas where the ground is unusually wet. If the ground is dry, the hammock can be set up as a small one-man tent.

The jungle hammock, however, has some limitations. Because it has free movement of air all around, it can be cold to sleep in during cool nights and downright miserable during cold weather. Also, like any hammock, it is tricky to get into. I have seen several campers

The jungle hammock, when suspended this way, is ideal for use in areas that have unusually wet ground. On dry ground, rig may be pitched as a small one-man tent.

flipped. Some fell out, and some found themselves lying on the inside of the upside-down roof and looking up at the inside of the hammock's bottom.

If you decide on a jungle hammock, practice putting it up and getting into and out of it at home before you take it on a camping trip. If you turn and toss at night, you may want to borrow a jungle hammock and try it out for a night or two before you decide whether to buy one. Hammock sleeping restricts movement and unusual sleeping positions and is not for every camper's comfort. But, if you can adjust to the jungle hammock's limitations, you'll find it a good swamp shelter for summer use.

The most practical swamp shelter is the tent. Many good tents on today's market are suitable for swamp camping. The basic qualities to look for in a tent for use in the swamp are that it is flame-resistant, has nylon screens over doors and windows, goes up easy, has a strong and moisture-resistant floor, and is made by a reputable manufacturer.

For boat or canoe travel, I use the Coleman "Compact Classic" tent. It is high enough, 5 feet, for me to dress in, and it is large enough for two adults to sleep comfortably along with any gear they want protected. The Classic is easy and fast to put up. When it's packed, it fits neatly in my canoe or boat.

When I travel by four-wheel-drive vehicle during cold weather in swamps, I use a Camel "Alamo" cabin tent. This tent is roomy (9 x 12 feet) and is excellent where weight and compactness are not limited. The Alamo sleeps four adults. When a Coleman Catalytic heater is added, the tent makes a nice base camp for duck hunting or deer hunting.

When you camp along a swamp river, you often will find your best campsites on sandbars. Then the best tent is one of the self-supporting dome tents which are commonly called pop tents. The one I use is manufactured by Sunshine Cover and Trap, Inc. Others are manufactured by American Eco Systems, Inc., North Face, and Early Winters, Ltd. Since there are no trees on most of the sandbars and the loose sand will often refuse to hold a tent peg, the self-supporting pop tents are a good choice for shelter. It is also worthy of note that these tents go up fast, making a quick shelter during a sudden rain shower. As with other tents, it is advisable to place a plastic cover under the pop tents. It will protect the tent floor from the grinding action of the sand, as well as from moisture. An added advantage these tents have is their shape. The dome shape allows them to withstand wind, and sandbars sometimes get plenty.

The tent you select for swamp camping deserves proper care. The wet environment can destroy a good tent fast. The first rule of tent camping in a swamp is to select as dry a campsite as possible. Next, always use a ground sheet of heavy plastic that's cut to the size of your tent floor. After removing all sticks and stones from your tent site, lay down the plastic ground cover. Then put your tent over the plastic. The plastic sheet will serve as a moisture barrier for your tent floor.

Make it a habit to clean out your tent every day. Not only will this practice give you a longer tent life but it will also help keep out unwanted pests. I have found that a small car broom will do the job nicely. Also make it a practice to keep the tent doors closed except when you go in and out. Then you'll be surprised at how few insects you'll have in the tent.

At the end of each camping trip, clean and dry your tent thoroughly. If you will follow this simple rule, a good tent becomes a long-term investment. Many swamp campers have ruined good tents by storing them damp and dirty, only to find several months later that the fabric has mildewed and is beginning to rot.

Sleeping Bag—The next item to put in your swamp bedroom is a good sleeping bag. The mystery of sleeping-bag insulation has confused campers for many years. In order to solve that mystery, let's look at a few facts about insulation.

What is insulation? The best insulation known is dead air. The human body loses heat when warm air moves away from it and cooler air moves toward it. In order to stay warm, we must stop this movement of air. When air is chopped up into small pockets and its movement has stopped, it is known as dead air. And dead air is what holds heat. The insulating fillers we find in garments and sleeping bags are not the actual insulation. They are only a means of chopping up the air, stopping air movement, and creating dead air.

Tests have shown that many materials (from steel wool to down) provide the same insulating qualities when the equal amount of material was used for the same thicknesses. Conclusions are that insulation depends on thickness of dead air. This thickness of insulation is called loft.

Insulation for sleeping bags has been made from materials that range from newspapers to steel wool. But the three most effective insulating fillers are Dacron Hollofil II, PolarGuard, and duck or goose down. In order that you may decide which insulation is best for your swamp-camping sleeping bag, let's examine each one.

Several years ago, Du Pont developed Dacron Hollofil II, a man-made fiber known as Dac II, as an insulating filler for outdoor garments and sleeping bags. The Dac II filament is short and hollow, thus giving more loft per pound than other man-made fillers. Another advantage of Dac II is that, according to Du Pont, it absorbs only ¾ of 1 percent of its own weight in moisture. So even in the worst downpour or swamp conditions, Dac II still retains its warmth-holding loft.

Many campers could not care less about how small a sleeping bag will compress. All they want is something that will keep them warm. But the campers who backpack or canoe into their favorite areas have found that sleeping bags which compress into a small bundle are a blessing. The backpack and canoe has limited space, so the smaller a sleeping bag will compress the better.

Dac II does not compress into a stuff sack as well as down, but it does compress as well as—if not better than—other synthetic fibers. If we use equal weights of goose down and Dac II and compress them with equal pressure, a sleeping bag filled with Dac II will compress about 90 percent as effectively as down.

Another comparison: about 1.4 pounds of Dac II is needed to give loft over the sleeper equal to the loft of 1 pound of goose down. Assuming equivalent construction and fabrics, a bag filled with 2 pounds of down would be replaced by a bag filled with 2.8 pounds of Dac II.

I have found only one disadvantage in my 2 years of using Dac II gear. If a sleeping bag or jacket is torn, the short fibers will pull out, leaving an area without insulation. A good example is the coon or grouse hunter whose sport takes him into thick brush. If he should rip the back of his jacket and lose its filler, he is without insulation over a large area of his body. Heat loss begins immediately.

Since Dac II is a short fiber, many outdoorsmen have been concerned that the fibers would leak out through the weave in the outer shell. I have not seen this happen in garments and sleeping bags made by reputable manufacturers. These companies use 1.9 ounce ripstop nylon, Gore-Tex, or 60/40 cloth as outer shells. These high-quality fabrics are found on Dac II, down, and PolarGuard items, and they do an excellent job of containing short or loose insulation such as Dac II and down.

Dac II has the added advantage of being machine washable, provided you follow the instructions. Cost of name-brand Dac II sleeping bags are within most outdoor families' budgets. A 3-pound Dac II sleeping bag costs around $60. It makes an excellent sleeping bag for swamp camping.

Another new man-made fiber that is making news as an insulating filler for outdoor gear is PolarGuard, made by the Celanese Corporation. PolarGuard is a solid, continuous polyester fiber that is lightly bonded with an acrylic resin. In order to learn more about PolarGuard, I talked with Dyke Williams, co-owner of the Country Ways Kit Company in Minnetonka, Minnesota. Williams probably has spent more time field-testing PolarGuard than anyone in the business. The following is his report.

"The Fortrel polyester fibers in PolarGuard are each several feet long. They are crimped into wiggles like ribbon candy and then woven into an interlocked blanket or batt which need only be sewn into the edge seams to keep it in place. No quilting or compartments are necessary—it won't sag or shift or bunch up.

"PolarGuard will keep you warm even if it is damp or wet. The fibers absorb less than 1 percent moisture. It has 83 percent more loft than down when wet. It is *very* resilient—keeping loft (and thus the insulating dead air

spaces) when wet, when slept upon, and when com-
pressed by other garments, and so on.

"You can wash and dry PolarGuard things anywhere,
by hand or tumble-action machine, and it dries extremely quickly. It doesn't leak out of accidental tears
or holes, and it is equally forgiving in sewing if you miss
a stitch or two. It's nonallergenic. It doesn't mildew.
PolarGuard doesn't need downproof covering materials
and so the nondownproof fabrics we use with it are up
to ten times more breathable, allowing body moisture to
escape and your comfort to remain."

PolarGuard has two disadvantages. First, like Dac II,
more PolarGuard than down is needed to provide the
same amount of loft, which means more weight to
carry. The second disadvantage is that PolarGuard does
not compress easily.

Cost of name-brand PolarGuard sleeping bags is
competitive with Dac II. And like Dac II, PolarGuard is
an excellent insulation for swamp-camping sleeping
bags.

The third and best-known insulating fiber is not
man-made. It is down, the part of the plumage on a
bird that is found closest to its skin. Commercial down
is a by-product of harvesting geese and ducks for food.
Down provides better insulation for less weight than
any other material.

Many people ask, "Which is best, goose or duck
down?" Today, since commercially raised geese are
smaller than the commercial geese of several years ago,
there is little difference except for the size of down
clusters in the two birds, provided they came from the
same climate and had the same diet. Goose down is only
slightly more efficient than duck down.

The ability of down to compact and spring back again
(resilience) is one of the most desirable traits of a down

bag or garment. The down-filled item can be compacted into a small space, smaller than a synthetic, and with a light shaking will spring back.

A major disadvantage of down is its cost. U.S. consumption of down reached over 17 million pounds in 1976. This was 175 percent over the 1975 figures. Along with the greater usage came higher prices. Good-grade down went from $7.50 a pound to over $25 and is still rising. A 3-pound down sleeping bag will cost you $130 or more.

Another disadvantage of down is that campers with an allergy cannot use down-filled equipment. They must use equipment filled with man-made fibers.

Down, when dry, is a champion among insulating materials. But when it gets wet, it has the reputation of collapsing and leaving the wearer in a dangerous situation.

Several years ago, I was hunting in the mountains on the North Carolina-South Carolina line. The temperature was just a degree or two above freezing, and rain was falling. Driving my four-wheel-drive vehicle along an narrow logging road, I was caught in a mud slide and found myself hopelessly stuck. Knowing that our base camp was just a couple of miles away in a gorge, I violated one of the basic rules of survival: I decided to walk to camp. I put on my down jacket and set out toward camp in the freezing downpour. I hadn't gone a quarter of a mile before I was soaked to the skin and the down jacket had lost all its loft. It was hard to believe. This was the same jacket that had kept me warm at 10°F. below zero the month before when I was hunting mule deer in Colorado. I still don't recall staggering into the Carolina camp, and it took my hunting companions several hours to reverse my case of hypothermia.

Down is good in dry cold but not in wet cold. Down and water don't mix. With this fact in mind, the swamp camper should avoid the use of down sleeping bags.

Perhaps more people are misled each year in buying sleeping bags than in the purchase of any other outdoor gear. Not long ago, I was on a trip when I saw a rental truck parked in front of a vacant service station. A large crowd was gathered around the back of the truck. Upon closer investigation I saw a sign that read, "Sleeping Bags $5 to $20."

Not being able to pass up a bargain, I stopped. None of the bags had filler tags attached. Those that were in the "down" pile had Rhode Island Red feathers working out of the loosely sewn seams. The zippers were terrible. The deal was a rip-off! But at the rate the uninformed buyers were hauling the bags off, it was a very successful rip-off for the seller.

Rule number one for buying sleeping bags is to buy from a reputable dealer who handles brand-name equipment.

The second rule is to decide on how much insulation you need for your camping. This varies from person to person. The best solution is to rent a quality sleeping bag and try it on your next camping trip. Then adjust up or down in insulation. If you are a winter camper as well as a summer camper, you may want to consider a heavier sleeping bag, leaving it unzipped for warm-weather use. The amount of insulation is a difficult area in which to make recommendations, and each camper must make his own choice based on his own comfort range.

Rule number three is to not let someone talk you into a backpack bag if you aren't a backpacker. Mummy bags have a place in backpacking, but they are not necessary for boat and vehicle camping. I find that I sleep much more comfortably in a full-size sleeping bag that has a zipper across the lower end and up one full side. On hot nights, I leave the bag unzipped and pull the top over me as the night cools. Also I find the full-size bag gives me more room for moving my legs around.

Buy your sleeping bags cautiously. Accept only Dac II or PolarGuard for insulation. Use rental bags until you find a bag that best suits you and your swamp-camping conditions.

Once you get a good sleeping bag, take care of it. Air it daily when you're in camp. This airing will help to counteract moisture buildup, a common occurrence in high-humidity swamps.

Mattresses—No swamp bedroom is complete without a mattress, and—in my opinion—no sleeping bag is comfortable without one. Today's market is flooded with mattresses of all types, designed to give the camper a good night's rest. There are foam mattresses, air mattresses, Ensolite pad mattresses, and combinations of these.

Most outdoorsmen who spend many days camping each year prefer the air mattress, especially if they are traveling by canoe or boat. I agree with their choice. The air mattress with the attached inflatable pillow is conducive to sound rest. The secret to getting maximum comfort out of an air mattess is to inflate it properly. Put only enough air in it so that when you sit on it your bottom can feel the ground. This way when you stretch out, it absorbs your weight. Many campers put into the mattress all the air it will hold and spend the night trying to stay on the hard bouncy mattress. Also be sure and carry a good patching kit. A puncture in the mattress can put you to thinking of home quickly.

Campers who prefer a foam mattress should heed the caution given by Byron Almquist, a Louisian swamp outfitter. Byron states that the open-celled foam pad or mattress should be avoided as it will absorb moisture like a sponge. Closed-cell foam mattresses should be full length and have a cover with a nylon bottom. This arrangement will protect the mattress, and a removable cover can be periodically cleaned.

I have guided campers who insisted on carrying cots. Cots are all right during warm weather and where there is room for their bulk. But if you're traveling by boat, cots should be avoided. Also remember that on cool nights, especially if there is any wind, a cot can be difficult to insulate and therefore is likely to allow you to get cold.

For most swamp conditions, the best air mattress is of quality construction and has a pillow. It packs easily (especially important if you are traveling by boat or canoe), is comfortable, and is relatively inexpensive.

This completes your swamp bedroom. A good tent, a full-size sleeping bag filled with Dac II or PolarGuard, and a good air mattress are the ingredients for restful nights in the swamp.

THE SWAMP KITCHEN

The equipment you select for your swamp kitchen will dictate, to some degree, how well you will eat during your stay. The first choice you must make is the source of heat on which to cook. Many of us who are from the old school still like to cook over an open fire when conditions allow it. But I must admit it's handy to use a stove fueled by liquid gas or propane.

The size of the stove you select will depend somewhat on the number of people you'll serve and the type food you choose to cook. For a group of two to four people who are using freeze-dried food, a one-burner stove will do the job in almost no time. If, however, you have a larger group or your group wants to cook fresh foods, then you'll need a two-burner or three-burner stove.

If most of your swamp travels will be done by boat or canoe, I would suggest that you try the Coleman Peak 1 one-burner camp stove, which uses liquid fuel. This small stove, coupled with a menu of freeze-dried food, will take up little space in your craft. A weekend's supply of food will weigh next to nothing.

If you'll travel by four-wheel-drive vehicle, you can choose one of the larger stoves fueled by liquid gas or propane. As with most outdoor equipment, stay with name brands and learn how to use the equipment in your backyard before you take a trip into the swamp.

A cook kit should be selected to match the size of your stove. A small kit containing two pots and one

A one-burner stove serves admirably for a group of two to four swamp campers who are using freeze-dried foods. Choose a stove that meets your party's needs.

frying pan will do well with a one-burner stove. If you plan on larger meals for larger groups, then select a larger cook kit. I recommend that you take your wife along when buying a cook kit. It's amazing how much she's likely to know about what utensils to buy and whether the kit is easy to clean.

If you yearn for a meal over an open fire, then you may want to consider America's oldest cook kit—the Dutch oven. I have seen them used in swamps from northern North America to many places in South America, and I don't think I've eaten a bad meal out of one yet.

The Dutch oven was invented, out of necessity, by early American settlers. Since most of their cooking was done outdoors or in a fireplace, they needed a pot that could do all the things a stove could do—bake, boil, fry, and broil. Thus, the first crude cast-iron Dutch oven was invented.

It is said that the final perfection of the Dutch-oven design was done by the famous Paul Revere, a skilled craftsman. This design is still used today.

Once the cast-iron pot became popular, it was produced in large numbers by New England manufacturers. It was not uncommon for Dutch traders to stop by the manufacturers to buy many of the pots for trading with the Indians. Thus the pot became known as the "Dutch" oven.

Today the true Dutch oven can be bought in some hardward stores, Boy Scout supply dealers, outdoor-equipment mail-order houses, or direct from the Lodge Manufacturing Company, South Pittsburg, Tennessee 37380.

The first-time buyer of a Dutch oven should make sure he is getting the real thing. It is made of heavy cast iron and has a flat bottom with three legs about 2 inches long. It has a strong bail. The lid is made of the same heavy material as the pot, and the lid has a small handle in the center. The lid's rim is flanged so that hot coals will stay on top while cooking. The Dutch oven is available in several sizes, usually from 8 to 16 inches in diameter and from 4 to 6 inches deep. The 12-inch diameter is the most popular size for family cooking. The cost ranges from $15 to $32, the weight from 7 to 30 pounds.

A word of caution: many modern-day flat-bottomed pots (no legs) are called Dutch ovens. They should be avoided as they are not designed for cooking on an open fire. It is also advisable to buy a round cake rack made from wire that will fit into your Dutch oven. The

The camper's Dutch oven (note flanged lid, bail, and legs) works best with proper accessories: wire cake rack for inside, folding shovel for moving hot coals, and hooked poker for moving hot coals and lifting oven by bail or lid by handle.

rack makes cleanup easier and will give a better baking job by keeping foods from sticking to the bottom of the oven.

The first step after you buy a Dutch oven is the most important one—breaking it in. The method most often used to break one in is to nearly fill the oven with good cooking oil and have a fish fry. From then on, try not to wash the pot with soapy water. The Dutch oven will usually wipe clean without any strong detergents or scrubbing. (For more about the Dutch oven, see Chapter 3.)

Another important piece of equipment you will need for your swamp kitchen is a water container. These days few swamps have safe drinking water. On the market are a number of good water containers such as

Swamp camper's water carriers can be store-bought containers or recycled plastic bottles. If you choose plastic bottles, be sure to clean them first according to detailed directions in this chapter.

those made by the Igloo Corporation. But for trips where boat or canoe transportation is used, I prefer to recycle the empty containers in which everything from bleach to bottled water is sold. These tough, durable plastic containers—after being thoroughly cleaned out and then filled with pure water—are easily stored in the canoe or boat and can take a lot of abuse without losing a drop of water.

Caution: if you choose to use any of these containers, follow these directions before filling a container with drinking water.

1. Shake a hot detergent solution inside the bottle.
2. Rinse thoroughly.
3. Wash with a baking-soda solution.
4. Rinse thoroughly.

You now have an excellent water-storage container. Mark "Drinking Water" on its side to let all know its purpose.

A swamp kitchen is not complete without a dining fly (sometimes called an overhead tarp). Cooking in the rain is not fun, and most swamps receive rain quite frequently. So the addition of a large nylon fly can make your camp much more livable. Not only does it protect you during periods of rain but it also provides shade during the heat of the day. Serving meals under the tarp, especially during rainy periods, will help keep your tent cleaner as well as bug-free.

So there you have your swamp kitchen complete with stove, cook kit, Dutch oven, water-storage containers, and a dining fly. All you need to add is a match and food. We will do that in the next chapter.

THE SWAMP BATHROOM

The swamp bathroom should contain your toothbrush, toothpaste, soap, face cloth, towel, comb, and whatever other necessities you use at home to keep yourself clean and healthy. It is a gross misconception that you must get as grimy as possible in order to be a camper. You will enjoy swamp camping much more if you have clean teeth and body. If you are on an extended trip, a sponge bath or even an occasional skinny dip will make you feel like a new person.

An essential part of your bathroom gear should be a toilet kit. There are two types you should consider, depending upon the type of campsite you may choose. If you will be camping on high ground, make a toilet kit

Here's the essential toilet kit to carry if you'll camp on a swamp's high ground. In an area that's usually wet, take along a portable toilet.

for your camp consisting of a garden trowel and a roll of toilet tissue stored in a waterproof plastic bag. When nature calls, select a suitable screened spot at least 50 feet from any open water or the campsite. Dig a hole 8 to 10 inches in diameter and no deeper than 6 to 8 inches. Fortunately, nature has provided in the top 6 to 8 inches of soil, a system of biological disposers that work to decompose organic material. Keep the sod intact if possible. After use, fill the hole with loose soil and then tramp in the sod. Nature will do the rest in a few days.

If you are going into an area that is usually wet, take along a portable toilet (available from Laacke & Joys, Milwaukee, Wisconsin). This portable toilet uses disposable bags, and you can bring the waste out with your other trash. A portable toilet of this type is required for all camping in the Okefenokee Swamp.

In short, your swamp bathroom serves the same purpose as your bathroom at home: it keeps you clean and healthy.

Now that we have the equipment for our swamp home, let's look at some of the miscellaneous equipment that you will need to make your swamp camp complete.

CLOTHING AND PROPER DRESS

The wet environment of the swamp requires that you wear the proper clothing, especially during the winter. Most people think of swamps as being hot and humid. This is somewhat true during the summer months, but it is not true during the winter, even in the Deep South.

For warm-weather swamp camping, this type of jungle boot is the best all-around footwear. It has canvas uppers, leather "feet," and lug soles.

Footwear—During the warm months, swamp campers have been seen wearing all types of footwear or none at all. While your activity will somewhat dictate what you wear, I have found that under most swamp conditions the so-called Viet Nam Jungle Boot is the best all-around footgear. This canvas-top, leather-foot boot has lug soles and is designed to keep your feet as dry as possible. The jungle boot is lightweight, gives your legs protection from mosquitoes and briers, and dries quickly.

I have found that these boots are reasonably priced at most army-navy stores. Except when I'm backpacking, I carry a spare pair of jungle boots into the swamps and keep them dry for wear around camp.

A summer swamp camp is no place for tennis shoes

or moccasins. Your exposed ankles would make good targets for insects and briers. And in the unlikely event that a snake decided to pay you a visit, your unprotected ankles would be vulnerable. Most seasoned swamp campers make wearing boots the rule rather than the exception during the warm months.

Cold-season footgear for swamp camping varies from one part of the country to another. The two boots I see most experienced "swampers" using are the L.L. Bean Maine Hunting Shoe (both the insulated and uninsulated styles) and the insulated rubber boot such as those made by Royal Red Ball and Sorel. Duck hunters, of course, wear waders, and hunters who stay on high-and-dry areas in the swamp wear their usual hunting boots. The important thing to remember is to keep your feet dry and avoid places where your boots will fail to give you proper protection from the cold.

Dressing To Stay Cool—Dressing to stay comfortable in the swamp during warm months is relatively easy if you follow a few basics. Starting at the top: always wear a hat of some type. The exposed head leads to discomfort from heat, bugs, or rain. The shirt and pants you select should be lightweight, made of a material that dries quickly, and (for insect protection) not be brightly colored. You should also wear a long-sleeved shirt and long pants for protection from sunburn and insects. If the conditions are favorable, you can always roll up your sleeves or shed the shirt. Many first-time swamp campers have a bad experience because they go into a swamp dressed as though they were on their way to a beach party. My favorite attire for summer swamp living is a camouflage suit that is made from 50 percent cotton and 50 percent polyester. It doesn't attract too many flying critters. And if I must get out of the boat to pull it over a log, the outfit then dries quickly.

Most swamps during the warm months are subject to rain showers. Several years ago, I noticed that when I got soaked by a sudden rainstorm, the mosquitoes and deer flies moved in by the hundreds for the feast. Then I began carrying a rain suit. I found that by staying as dry as possible I eliminated much of the insect problem. Mosquitoes like warm, wet objects, so carry a rain suit. Not only will you be more comfortable in general by staying dry but you will also be less bothered by insects. Be sure the rain suit you select has vents so that the moisture from your body can escape. One made of Gore-Tex is "breathable." A cheap, unvented rain suit can get you soaked from within by keeping your body's moisture trapped inside the suit.

Where insects are extremely bad, a head net is an advisable item to pack in your camping gear. Many times, fishing would be misery without a head net.

Contrary to the belief of many campers, the swamp, even in the Sun Belt during warm weather, can get uncomfortably cool at night. One of my most miserable nights in the outdoors was an August night I spent, unexpectedly, in a South Carolina swamp. I was totally unprepared, and I shook from cold all night. It was a welcome sun I greeted the next morning. Always take a windbreaker and warm shirt into the swamp with you. No matter how hot the days may get, some nights a light breeze will cool the swamp quickly—and you with it unless you're properly dressed.

Dressing To Stay Warm—As I stated earlier, it's much more of a challenge to stay comfortable in a swamp during the cold months.

In order to learn how to stay warm in the swamp during the winter we must first understand our source

In order to stay warm in a swamp during the winter, you must understand the relationship between body heat and the various ways of preventing its loss. Credit: Tom Gresham.

of body heat and the ways in which we lose this valuable heat.

Humans, like all mammals, must maintain a stable body temperature. When we are away from external sources of heat, our only heat source is that which is produced inside our bodies. This inner warmth comes chiefly from burning food, the oxidation of carbohydrates. Carbohydrates, our major source of warmth, are easily digested and provide fast energy for muscles, nerves, and brain. The body does not store them for future use because they are burned within a short period of time and must be replenished often if we are to stay warm. Carbohydrates are readily available to us in raisins, chocolate, candy, sugar, fruits, and breads.

Now that we know our source of body heat, let's notice how we lose this warmth. There are five ways you can get cold. These heat "robbers" are known as conduction, radiation, convection, evaporation, and respiration. The loss of heat by respiration is the only one of the five that we have little or no control over. The air we breathe on a cold day enters cold and leaves warm. The body heat consumed in heating this air is beyond our control since we cannot stop breathing.

If you sit on a metal tree stand or hold a gun in your bare hand, you thereby lose heat. Both metal objects are cold, and heat flows from you to them. Heat flow is from warm objects to cold. This heat loss is known as conduction. If your clothing gets damp with sweat when you walk into a swamp, heat flows by conduction from your skin to the cold, wet clothing.

Never go into the outdoors in the winter without a hat. Your head is the only part of your body where blood vessels do not constrict to conserve heat. They must supply the brain to insure its proper functioning. Winter-survival experts estimate that 15 to 50 percent of the body's total heat production may be lost through an unprotected head. This type of heat loss is known as radiation.

Dressing for a cold day in the swamps in clothing made of cotton and synthetics is dangerous. There's practically nothing to stop the movement of cold air from washing away your warmth. The horizontal motion of air around your body creates a wind-chill factor that can move body-surface warmth away and replace it with cold air faster than the body can rewarm it. This heat loss is known as convection.

If you exert much effort at all in the swamp, chances are your clothing will get damp with sweat. You will be losing heat by evaporation. Although evaporation is the natural way the body cools itself, the process of sweating can have very dangerous consequences during cold weather. If you're improperly dressed, the clothing around your body absorbs the moisture. This moisture moves through the layers of clothing until it reaches a layer that is below what it called dew-point temperature. Here it condenses and wets the layer. Then the moisture wicks back to your skin. Sweat-soaked clothing causes rapid chilling of the skin. There's a big difference between the results of a healthy sweat of a long day of bass fishing and the sweat of winter. The winter sweat can lead to chills, frostbite, and hypothermia.

The best way to dress for a cold day in the swamp is to wear clothing that preserves your body heat while allowing body moisture to evaporate freely. This effect is accomplished through the principle of layering—in other words, wearing alternate layers of clothing that provide both insulation and ventilation.

Underwear, since it is worn next to your skin, should "breathe," allowing moisture to escape. Fishnet underwear is ideal for this purpose. This unique underwear

Wayne Fears models the elements in one system of dressing in layers: fishnet underwear, then a layer of wool (hunting shirt and trousers), and finally a jacket appropriate for the weather.

was first used by Scandinavian fishermen who discovered that they could stay warm by covering themselves with their dry nets. The idea has been refined down through the years. Today's fishnet underwear, having ⅜-inch-square mesh, will effectively allow moisture to escape out the neck opening rather than soak your clothing.

The second layer should be made of a wool hunting shirt and wool trousers. Wool has been overlooked for many years, especially in the South, as an insulating material. It is, nevertheless, an excellent insulator and insulates when wet better than any other fiber.

Have you ever considered the consequences of wearing a belt tightly around your waist to hold up your trousers? This practice restricts circulation and stops ventilation—two effects that cause you to get cold. Buy a pair of good suspenders, and keep your pants loose around the waist. You will stay warmer. Hunters in colder climates have been using this bit of lore for centuries.

The third layer of clothing should be a jacket of wool or a coat filled with Dac II or Polar-Guard. Unlike down, these two fillers will not totally lose their insulating value when they get wet. If you are hunting, you will want to consider a reversible coat, one that has Blaze Orange on one side and a camouflage pattern on the other.

The fourth layer is a rain suit. Wetness can be deadly in a swamp, so keep a rain suit handy.

One of the most important items of clothing you can wear is a cap or hat to protect your head. For cold weather, I prefer a Blaze Orange wool stocking cap, sometimes called a watch cap. If I get caught out in a cold rain or wind, I put on over the watch cap the waterproof hood of my rainsuit jacket. Not only is that hooded jacket good in the rain but it's also an excellent wind breaker. Whatever type of cap you choose, make sure it will protect your head in all types of cold weather. Make sure your cap can be pulled down to protect your ears. Since the head is a principal point of heat loss, covering it can warm other parts of the body. The mountain men had a saying: "When your feet are cold, put on your hat." There's a lot of truth in it.

The best way to keep your hands warm might be to wear wool mittens. But under hunting conditions and other swamp activities, this idea is not practical. The next-best hand protectors are wool gloves with a wind-proof shell over them. If you expect rain or wet conditions such as those you encounter in duck hunt-ing, an extra pair of wool gloves in your hunting-coat pocket could be a welcome relief.

The parts of us that seem to get coldest the fastest are our feet. This phenomenon is no accident. Our body is programmed to automatically regulate its warmth for survival. When cold conditions exist, the body adjusts its heat production and circulation to maintain life. When the body's core temperature drops slightly, the brain and central nervous system receive the highest priority. In order to keep these vital areas warm, the body curtails circulation to its extremities. The feet, being the farthest from the core, are the first to feel the reduced circulation. So a hat really can help keep your feet warm.

If you wear a hat and your body is properly protected by the layering system, there is little reason for your feet to be cold if they are adequately covered. Cold-weather foot covering should start with two pairs of wool socks. Since the feet are efficient producers of sweat, wool is required. Remember: it insulates even when wet. If wool next to your skin irritates you, wear a thin pair of silk or nylon socks next to your skin and then a pair of wool socks over them. If the weather is not too cold, you may want to wear only one pair of wool socks. When you put on your socks and boots, be very careful to eliminate all wrinkles. Sock wrinkles slow down blood circulation in the feet and toes, causing them to get cold. Always carry an extra pair of wool socks, especially if you do a lot of walking. Change socks when your feet get wet and cold.

Your leather boots should be kept water repellent with a wax-type compound like Sno-Seal. Greases and oils soak into the leather and reduce its natural insulating properties. Also be careful not to lace your boots too tight. Tightness can cut circulation and cause cold feet. Many seasoned hunters buy their cold-weather boots one size larger than normal to allow for comfortably wearing two pairs of wool socks.

If you're sitting on a deer stand, duck blind, or boat seat with your feet properly covered and you still have cold feet, ask yourself a few questions:

Are your feet wet?

Are you properly dressed in layers?

Do you have on warm head gear?

Are your boots too tight or socks wrinkled?

Are the clothes on your legs too tight? Is the way you're sitting cutting off the circulation in your legs?

The answers to these questions can help you keep your feet warm.

When you're properly dressed, how do you stay warm under swamp conditions that involve walking awhile and sitting awhile?

The first rule is to avoid sweating. All winter clothing should be loose fitting. If you wear fishnet underwear as your first layer of clothing, a great deal of body moisture will be forced out around your neck opening by the "bellows" action of your loose clothing. When you walk, maintain a slow pace; avoid working up a heavy sweat. As you begin to feel warm walking, take the following action as needed to stay comfortable and avoid overheating:

1. Take your gloves off.
2. Unzip your jacket.
3. Remove your hat.
4. Take off your jacket.

When you sit down, begin to replace those items as you cool off. Once you get accustomed to the tricks of maintaining constant warmth without sweating, you'll be amazed at how comfortable you can stay on a cold day.

As I mentioned at the beginning of this section, carbohydrates are the inner source of our warmth. Since this "fuel" cannot be stored during cold-weather hunting conditions, it is necessary to replenish it during a cold day's hunt. Keep a few high-energy food bars or nonmelting chocolate candy in your hunting-coat pocket. Throughout the day, nibble along. You will be keeping fuel in the body's furnace. If you are worried about calories, it may help you to know that a human needs about 4,000 calories to maintain optimum strength and ability to walk-hunt all day.

Swamp travelers who backpack or camp during cold weather should never sleep in the clothes they wear during the day. During the night, your body is renewing its energy supply and a lot of moisture is given off. This moisture will be absorbed in the clothes and the camper will start out with damp clothing. This is why seasoned outdoorsmen generally sleep in the nude and air their sleeping bags daily. Without this airing, the sleeping bag will stay damp and cold.

Cold-weather hunting can be dangerous to anybody who fails to take the time to learn the woodsman's art of staying warm. Hypothermia kills a few swamp campers every year. Wintertime swamp conditions can cause frostbite. But if for no other reason than to be a skilled camper, you should learn to stay warm.

Learn how to stay warm and camp during the cold days. Fewer campers will be around to crowd you; there will be no snakes, ticks, or mosquitoes to bother you; and you will have the satisfaction of knowing that you have come one step closer to being a master swamp camper.

KNIVES AND OTHER CUTTING TOOLS

Today's campers have been oversold on the belief that it takes a knife with a $100-plus price tag on it to be any good. This just isn't so. True, the high-priced knives are of top quality and are a thing of beauty, but how many of us noncollectors are willing to pay a lot of money for a good working knife?

If we look back in history to the late 1700s during Daniel Boone's time, we see a group of backcountry explorers known as "long hunters." These men depended upon their knives daily for defense, skinning bears, cleaning fish, and doing homestead chores. Their knife wasn't a high-priced custom-made model. It was simple and looked like a homemade butcher knife. But it got them through a tough era of history.

Our modern camping knives have come a long way since the days of the long hunters. Today we can choose an expensive collector's item or a less-expensive but high-quality hunting knife. In fact, for less than $30 a camper can get a good working knife for most all camping purposes.

I like the under-$30 price tag for several reasons. The most obvious reason, of course, is that I don't have to spend a week's worth of grocery money before I can skin a deer. The second reason is that over the years I have managed to lose several knives. I left one on a stump in the Okefenokee Swamp. I left another at a spring in the mountains of Tennessee. A third was borrowed from my truck by an unknown borrower. I was sorry to lose these knives, but I knew it wouldn't break me to replace them. The third and perhaps most important reason I like these lower priced knives is that most of them—if selected from a reputable manufacturer of known quality—will do anything within reason that an expensive knife will do and you won't care if it gets scratched or dirty.

What are we looking for in a good camping knife? First of all we want a knife made from a high-carbon steel that's been hardened and tempered for a long-lasting edge. Since most of us aren't metallurgists, we must take a manufacturer's word or get advice from a friend who has been using a similar knife. So it's important to buy from a reputable manufacturer whose advertising you can believe and who will guarantee the knife.

The second thing to look for in a camping knife is quality construction. Nobody wants a knife whose handles fall off the first time you use it. Again, this hazard can be avoided by staying with the reputable brands.

The third factor to consider is size. How often have you spotted a camper who had seen too many Western movies and had bought a 3-pound 12-inch Bowie knife? If you are going to defend the Alamo, that's all right; but for general outdoor use, forget it. A 3- to 4-inch blade will do the job.

The fourth factor to consider is one that causes knife buffs to call me another nasty name: what blade design is best for camping use? I think this is a matter of personal preference. Many big-game hunters prefer the drop-point blade while others prefer the clip blade. Some trappers prefer the skinning blade, and others prefer to sheepfoot. Take your time and think about what you want the knife to do. Experience will be your best guide to blade design.

And then there's the question of which type of knife you want to carry. Should it be the type with a fixed blade (commonly called a belt knife) or a folding knife? There are strong and weak arguments for each. The fixed-blade knife is stronger because it has no moving parts. On the other hand, the folding knife takes up less room and is easier to wear on the belt when getting into and out of vehicles, canoes, and boats. The lock-blade folding knife is illegal to carry in some states. On the other hand, the fixed-blade knife on your belt will bring about stares of distrust in some areas. Both designs are good. What counts more than anything else is your preference. It is my opinion that if you choose a folding knife for general outdoor use, you should get one with a lock blade. I carry a scar from a nonlock folding knife that folded when I had my hands inside a deer cutting.

My choice of an all-around knife for use in swamp camping is a lock folding knife. Not only is it convenient to carry but it will also do just about anything the fixed-blade belt knife can do. I have used lock folding knives made by Schrade, Normark, Gutmann, and Precise with a great deal of satisfaction. These knives are well made, contain good steel, and are relatively inexpensive.

A second cutting tool that I find most useful in swamp camping is the army-surplus machete. This

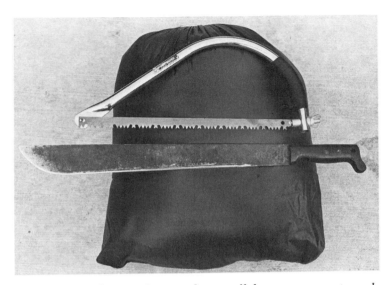

An army-surplus machete and a small bowsaw are extremely helpful cutting tools in various swamp-camping situations.

inexpensive long (24-inch) knife does a good job clearing campsites, cutting firewood, and opening up boat trails. It also packs well in my canoe and four-wheel-drive vehicle.

The third cutting tool I use when firewood is a must, or when a trail must be opened up in a swamp, is a camp saw made by True Temper, Inc. This saw has a 15-inch blade that will cut through a 4-inch log in almost no time and packs easily.

With a good knife, machete, and camp saw, the swamp camper can do almost any wood cutting or camp chore necessary. The four-wheel-drive camper may want to throw in a good pole ax or small chain saw, but they really aren't necessary unless you must cut enough wood to keep a Maine deer camp warm for a week.

WATERPROOF MATCHES—A MUST

One of the most important items a swamp camper should have with him at all times are kitchen matches in a waterproof container. I stress kitchen matches because this 2½-inch-long strike-anywhere wooden match can be ignited easily and burns long enough to get a fire going.

You can waterproof kitchen matches by dipping the match head and a ½-inch of the stem into melted paraffin or by painting the same area with fingernail polish. However, don't treat the whole match, as the flame will run down to your fingers after the match is struck. You can make a very good waterproof match container by putting kitchen matches (you must cut off ¼ inch of stem) in a plastic 35-mm film container. The lid seals the matches in watertight.

There are several good commercially made waterproof match containers available at most outdoor and sporting-goods stores. The one that most survival experts like is made from a Blaze Orange plastic and has a compass on one end and a whistle on the other.

Regardless of what type of waterproof container you have, don't pack your matches too tightly. If you do, you can't get them out when you need them. Include a small birthday candle, preferably one of those trick candles that you can't blow out. This makes a good emergency fire starter. It is a wise camper who has several waterproof match containers in his camp gear. I always carry one with me, one in my cook kit, one in my canoe, and one in my vehicle.

FIRST-AID KITS

First-aid kits come in all shapes and sizes. The two that I have used with a great deal of satisfaction are the Trail-Aid Kit by Survival Systems, Inc. and the Travel Pack by Cutter Laboratories. These kits carry the basic first-aid supplies in a kit form that packs well. In snake country, I always carry a snakebite kit with the first-aid kit. Most commercial first-aid kits do the job provided you are trained in first aid. I find that campers who have taken the Red Cross first-aid course usually are prepared for any emergencies that may arise on a camping trip.

WATERPROOF STORAGE BAGS

If you do much swamp exploring by boat or canoe, and you're bitten by the swamp-camping bug, odds are you will find that in order to keep your gear dry you must pack it in waterproof bags. Most swamp outfitters have tried using plastic household garbage bags at one time or another and wind up cussing them. These bags tear easily and won't last 2 days on the trail. For big items such as tents, sleeping bags, cooking gear, and so on, I use the large heavyweight canvas pack bag made by Sportspal Canoe Company.

For my cameras and clothes, I use the bags specially designed for these purposes by Phoenix Products, Inc. The camera bag has an inflated chamber around it to give the cameras extra protection. A sudden downpour or the splashing that accompanies getting in and out of the canoe in water can make these bags worth a lot to you at day's end when you have dry camping gear.

Keeping your clothing and camera and other gear dry is a critical part of swamp camping. Use the right combination of canvas and plastic bags.

LIGHTING THE SWAMP CAMP

Having lights in the swamp camp makes the experience much more enjoyable and safe, especially in snake country. Many excellent gasoline and propane lanterns are available to the camper. I see many campers who buy a new lantern and then fail to try it out until the first night in camp. Don't make this mistake. Lanterns (especially where the installation of mantles is concerned) are tricky, so learn how to use yours at home.

Also always carry spare mantles. I keep two spares taped to the bottom of my lantern so they will be there when needed.

You will also want to consider a lantern hanger to use in camp. An elevated lantern can light up an entire campsite, while a low lantern is somewhat limited. Good light is especially important when you prepare a meal. I was late getting into camp one night several years ago in Georgia's Alapaha River Swamp. The fish had been biting, and I forgot it was my night to cook. In a rush, I turned over a boat, sat a gas lantern on it, and used the boat bottom as a table. As I was mixing my hush-puppy batter, a swarm of mayflies covered the lantern and my batter as well. Knowing supper couldn't wait for new batter, I just kept stirring. My fishing pardners still talk of those hush puppies with wings. The funny part was they didn't notice the wings until the second helping. I could have avoided the fly hatch in my batter if I had taken the time to properly hang the lantern. A hung lantern is also out of danger of being kicked or knocked over.

During the mosquito season, I like to take along a couple of candle lanterns to hang around the dining tent. When citronella candles are burned in these handy little lanterns, the flying pests keep their distance. You get light plus mosquito protection.

For light in the sleeping tent or for walking around camp, you can't beat the little Mallory Duracell compact flashlight. Noted swamp outfitter Byron Almquist of the Canoe and Trail Shop in New Orleans puts a cord through the hole in this flashlight and wears it around his neck. He is never without light. He tells me this arrangement gives a reassuring feeling to first-time swamp campers. You can also hang up the light, freeing your hands to do a camp chore at night.

3

Food and Cooking

Food can make or break a camping experience. Somehow we seem to remember camps that had half-cooked food, spoiled food, or tasteless food. The chances of your having such an experience today have been greatly reduced by a relatively new method of food processing called freeze-drying.

FREEZE-DRIED FOODS

What happens in the processing plant is that meats and vegetables are quickly frozen down to −50°F. Next the frozen food is placed in a chamber where the pressure is rapidly reduced to almost vacuum conditions. In the freezing process, the water in the food changes from liquid to ice crystals, then directly from ice to water vapor. The result is what we call freeze-dried food.

The advantages of freeze-dried foods are many. They retain their true flavor, they reconstitute quickly, the food—to my eye—retains its look (whereas dehydrated foods look shriveled), few nutrients are lost since water is the only thing taken out of the food, and practically instant meals are possible because an entire meal can be cooked and then freeze-dried.

The major disadvantage of freeze-dried food is its fairly high cost. But for short camping trips into the swamps, the cost is well worth it. Freeze-dried food requires no refrigeration; is packaged in small premeasured servings; and is light in weight, requiring little storage space. Since most freeze-dried meals re-

Freeze-dried foods and selected foods from supermarket shelves make easy the preparation of tasty, nourishing meals in the swamp.

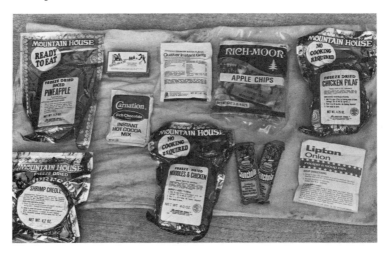

quire only boiling water, you gain time for hunting, fishing, or exploring. The freeze-dried dishes are varied, and the most finicky eater can find something to please his taste. These foods can be found in most backpack shops and outfitting stores.

Another source of fast camp meals is your supermarket's shelves. A growing number of freeze-dried, powdered, and dehydrated foods are being processed for home use. These foods, many the result of lessons learned in our space program, are nutritional, prepare fast, taste good, and weigh little. Some examples that I have tried are Lipton's Beef Stroganoff, Carnation Hot Cocoa Mix, Quaker Instant Oatmeal, Tang Orange Drink, Lipton Soups, Kraft Macaroni and Cheese, Jello Instant Pudding, and Borden's Instant Potatoes. The list could go on for several pages, but this is a sample of what's available.

The trick to using these lightweight store-bought foods is to repackage them at home in servings for one, two, or three persons. Use plastic bags, and be sure to label your bags and include any necessary directions. As you plan your menu for a camping trip, put the small bags with the ingredients for each meal into a larger plastic bag and label it accordingly—"Saturday-Breakfast for four." This will keep your meals organized and will cut down on meal-preparation time.

FRESH FOODS

Many campers prefer to take fresh foods on their forays into the swamp. This is a fine idea if the boat or vehicle has enough space. The chief concern for fresh foods, especially during warm months, is spoilage. Many good ice chests are on the market, and a block of ice in a well-insulated ice chest will last for a long time, provided the chest is kept in the shade and the lid is securely fastened. Use plastic bags to keep individual meats, fruits, and vegetables clean and fresh. Drain your ice chest frequently. Water at the bottom might ruin food that falls to the bottom, and the water is unnecessary weight. Keep your ice chest clean. Give it a thorough cleaning and airing between trips.

WILD FOODS

Many campers are showing a renewed interest in living off the land. This is a very refreshing approach but requires a good knowledge of plants and animals. It is not the purpose of this book to give you a course in eating from the land, but I do encourage hunters and fishermen to enjoy a part of their catch or kill in a camp meal. Fish can be cooked many ways in camp. So can small game and cuts from big game. This fresh meat can be a welcome change from packaged foods.

The one problem that many campers have with fresh fish caught during the summer is that it spoils very quickly unless kept on ice. If you are without ice, try this method of keeping fish fresh:

Keep in mind that the two enemies of fresh fish are heat and moisture. These elements make a good medium in which bacteria will grow, and bacteria causes spoilage. After catching a fish, clean it and wipe the body cavity with a cloth or paper towel. If you have used water in cleaning the fish, wipe both the body cavity and the outside, making sure it is dry. Hang the fish in a cool place, in much the same manner that you hang a deer on a hunting trip. A glaze will form on the fish. At night, hang the fish so they will cool, provided it is a cool night. During the day, wrap them in papers and cover them with blankets or even wrap them in sleeping bags to keep the heat of the day away. Once the fish are cool and dry, you can seal them in waterproof plastic bags and then cover the bags with wet cloth or burlap. The evaporation will cool them even more, yet they will not be touched by water, one of the enemies of fresh-caught fish.

The swamps are full of edible wild foods available to the trained outdoorsman. A good example is the crawfish. Unknown as a wild food to most campers outside the state of Louisiana, the crawfish is a rare delicacy that is found in most swamp waters. To catch them, cut two or three long poles. Attach 8 feet of fishline to each pole. That's all. No hooks needed. Tie a piece of raw meat, about 1-inch square, firmly on the end of each line. Throw the baited lines into the swamp water.

Approximately every 10 minutes carefully lift a pole until the bait is near the surface. If you have crawfish clinging to the bait, slip a landing net under them. Be careful not to raise the crawfish out of the water until the net is under them as they will get away. Drop your catch into a wet burlap bag. When you have enough for supper, heat a large pot of salted water to a brisk boil. Toss the crawfish in and simmer for 5 minutes only. Any more boiling will overcook these crustaceans. Next, drop the hot crawfish in some chilled water. As soon as they are cool, break off their tails, peel them, dip in ketchup, and eat a swamper's delight.

North American swamps offer a variety of berries, nuts, and other edible plant life. It behooves the swamp camper to learn the edible plants found in the swamps in his part of the country or in any swamp he goes into. It is surprising how much wild food a swamp offers.

TRAIL FOODS

Since most of our swamp camping involves travel and hard work, many of our noon meals are eaten while paddling a canoe, running a boat, or walking. Trail foods that you can make at home will give you a nutritious meal while you're on the go.

Jerky—Most of the early swamp explorers in North America found that they needed a lightweight nutritional trail food that required no special storage. From the Indians they learned how to make a trail food that met these requirements. It was called jerky. Today, those of us who enjoy backcountry activities have somewhat the same requirements as those of the earlier explorers—to travel light but eat good. We can still depend on homemade jerky.

Jerky can easily be made in your home oven. It makes a good rainy-Saturday project. Almost any lean cut of beef or venison can be made into jerky. The cheaper cuts such as round steak work as well as any. Jerky is pure protein, so you can eat as much as you can hold. It will give enduring energy. Yet jerky is free of carbohydrates, so it won't add pounds to your weight. Besides being an excellent trail food, jerky is good in stews. Simply mix the jerky into the pot with the rest of the stew ingredients. The jerky will quickly absorb moisture during cooking and will enlarge to become plump, tender pieces of meat.

To make jerky, cut the meat into strips 6 inches long

and about ½ inch wide and ¼ inch thick. Be sure to cut the strips with the grain running lengthwise. This detail keeps the jerky from breaking easily. Trim off all fat; otherwise it will turn rancid. Then season the strips with salt and pepper and brush on Liquid Smoke or a similar flavoring.

Stick a round toothpick through one end of each strip. Place a layer of aluminum foil in your oven to catch the drippings, and suspend the strips from the top oven rack. Turn the heat on to 120°F. (or the lowest temperature of your oven). Leave the oven door slightly open so that the moisture can escape. Heat for approximately 8 hours or until the meat has turned dark and there is no moisture in the center of the strip.

When the strips are done, they should be completely dry but flexible enough to bend without breaking. Remove the strips from the oven, take the toothpicks out, and store the jerky in a sealable plastic bag.

Pemmican—American Indians found that they could not live on jerky alone. It supplied only protein and had no fat and few vitamins. In order to balance their diet, the Indians melted animal fat and added crushed berries, nuts, and shredded jerky. The mixture was poured into bags made of animal membrane, and the cooled result was called pemmican.

Our history is rich in accolades to pemmican. Alexander MacKenzie cached pemmican in grass-lined and bark-lined holes in the ground for the return trip during his first crossing of North America. America's greatest hunting trip, the Lewis and Clark Expedition, depended upon pemmican as their trail food. Admiral Peary's successful journey to the North Pole was accomplished with pemmican as the staple food. Peary and his men ate it cold, twice a day. The admiral wrote that it was the "most satisfying food I know."

Throughout my years in the backcountry I have worked to find an improved pemmican recipe that incorporates modern-day foodstuffs. The following modern pemmican is the result of much trail testing.

Run twice through a food grinder one cup each of dried peaches, dried apples, raisins, dried prunes, coconut, and chopped peanuts. Bind them together by mixing in ½ cup each of the following: margarine, honey, and peanut butter. Press the mixture together into candy-bar-size portions and roll each bar in powdered sugar. Store the bars in sealed plastic bags in the freezer until you are ready to hit the trails.

I should point out here that the dried fruits in this recipe for modern pemmican are my choice. You may have other preferences, or you may want to eliminate some. Just be sure that whatever fruit you select is dried. You will also notice I elected *not* to add shredded jerky to my recipe, even though it was used in the Indians' pemmican. It's just a matter of opinion. I like jerky by itself and therefore do not put it in my pemmican. The decision is yours.

Granola—This snack can be eaten out of the hand or mixed with water to become a breakfast cereal.

You'll need the following ingredients for making granola: 1 cup of soy flour; 1 cup of shredded flaked coconut; 1 cup of chopped cashews; 1 cup of chopped almonds; 2 cups of wheat germ; 6 cups of rolled flakes (oat, barley, wheat, or rye); ½ cup of unhulled sesame seeds; 2 tablespoons of brewer's yeast; 1 teaspoon of salt; 1 cup of vegetable oil; 1 cup of honey; and 4 cups of dried fruit (such as apricots, prunes, dates, cherries, apples, and raisins).

In a large pot, mix all dry ingredients except the fruit. Pour honey and oil over all and mix well. Spread the mixture evenly on three 10 x 15 x 1-inch jelly pans. Bake in a slow (250°F.) preheated oven for 1½ hours or until the granola is as crunchy as you like. Stir every half hour for even baking. Then cool the granola.

Cut up dried fruit and mix it thoroughly into the granola. Spoon the result into plastic bags. Seal and store in the refrigerator.

Bannock—Bannock, bread (originally unleavened) of Scottish descent, has been the trail bread of the wilderness traveler for centuries. It's still very popular among people who spend most of their time in swamps.

I will give you the basic mix in one-man proportions. The mix can be put together in advance and will stay fresh for 6 weeks or more if kept covered, sealed, dry, and cool.

The basic ingredients for bannock are: 1 cup of all-purpose flour; ¼ teaspoon of salt; 1 teaspoon of double-action baking powder (not in original recipe); and 2 tablespoons of powdered skim milk.

Cooking the bread is simple. Add enough cold water to the bannock mix to make a soft dough. Mold this rapidly (with as little handling as possible) into a cake about 1 inch thick, and lay it in a hot greased pan. Hold the pan over the fire until a crust forms on the bottom of the bannock and then turn the dough over.

At this stage, prop the skillet at a steep angle in front of your fire so that the loaf will receive a lot of heat on top. When the bannock looks golden brown, test it by sticking a twig into the loaf. If the dough sticks, the loaf needs more heat. After you have cooked bannock awhile, you can tap it with your finger and gauge by the hollow sound when it is done. Cooking time is usually 15 minutes, more or less.

The basic mix may be varied in many ways. You can add fruits such as raisins and blueberries or spices such as cinnamon and nutmeg.

FOOD PROTECTION

One advantage of going into the swamps is the opportunity to see an abundance of wildlife. In many swamps, wild creatures have seen so few people that they don't necessarily show a fear of man. This is especially true where food is involved. Several years ago, two of us were making our way across the Okefenokee Swamp. The last night in the swamp was spent on Billy's Island. We were down to half a loaf of bread and some peanut butter for supper. I had spent the afternoon dreaming of peanut-butter sandwiches as we pushed our canoe through miles of lily pads. As we were setting up camp, a raccoon eased up to where we had laid our meager supplies. With a dash, the raccoon grabbed the bread and disappeared instantly into the brush. After a wild but fruitless chase, we settled down for a meal of straight peanut butter.

On another occasion, down in a south Florida swamp, I arose one morning and decided to pour myself a bowl of corn flakes for breakfast. I poured a squirrel out of the box instead.

Until I learned to put foodstuffs out of reach of animals, I was visited by bears, skunks, opossums, and a various assortment of swamp critters.

If I'm camping near my vehicle, I now make it a policy to store foodstuffs in it. But anybody who is backpacking or boating deep into the swamp is faced with a problem of storage. The method of storage I use under those conditions is one I picked up from watching swamp trappers. They take a cotton or nylon bag and put all their nonperishable foodstuffs in it. (Any food that is not wrapped so as to be waterproof should first be placed in a plastic bag, then put into the cotton or nylon bag.) Then they tie a long rope around the neck of the bag and throw the other end of the rope over a limb. They pull the bag to within 3 feet of the limb and tie the loose end of the rope around the trunk of the tree. This cache, as it is called, works well. I have been using it for years with no problems.

Here's the way to keep animals from getting into your supply of nonperishable foods: hoist it beyond their reach from the ground, the tree trunk, or the overhead branch. Same technique works for keeping garbage out of their clutches.

If you have perishable food items, it is best to store them in a strong ice chest with the lid fastened down tight.

COOKING OVER OPEN FIRES

As I watch a younger generation of campers try their hand at swamp camping, the more I realize that the art of what I call firemanship is dying. Usually they can't get a fire started. And if they do, they ordinarily don't know what to do with it.

Firemanship is a relatively simple skill to master. You clear out an area measuring 10 feet in diameter of all sticks, stones, and so on. If the ground is moist or wet, build a wooden platform by putting several dry sticks side by side. Next, find a supply of tinder. It may be "lighter" wood, old bird nests, dead lower branches of a hemlock, bark from a dead river birch, or bark from a dead cedar. Suitable tinder will vary depending on the part of the country you're camping in and on the area's conservation regulations. Next, get a good supply of small sticks and twigs. Then a supply of larger dead wood.

On your platform or ground if it is dry, place your tinder and small sticks over it in a tepee shape. Light the tinder, and slowly add slightly larger sticks until you have a fire going that can handle the larger wood.

Don't rush your fire. If you do, you are likely to smother it. If the swamp is so wet that finding dry wood is impossible, use a candle or can of Sterno under the tinder. This technique will help dry the small sticks and twigs quickly, allowing them to burn. Soon you can put on larger wood to dry. Dead standing trees are usually drier than down trees.

One word of caution. Never start a fire on peat moss or similar material. It can burn underground for several yards, starting a major swamp fire.

All campers should learn what trees make the best firewood in their camping area. By burning the best fuelwood, you can get a maximum efficiency from each log burned. The densest wood makes the best fuelwood for camp use. See the chart for densities of North American woods.

DENSITIES OF VARIOUS NORTH AMERICAN WOODS

HARDWOODS

High (Excellent)	*Medium* (Adequate)	*Low* (Fair)
Live Oaks	Sugar Maple	Red Alder
Eucalyptus	American Beech	Large Tooth Aspen
Hop Hornbeam	Honey Locust	Basswood
Dogwood	Yellow Birch	Chestnut
Hickory	White Ash	Catalpa
Shadbush	Elm	Black Willow
Persimmon	Black Gum	Box Elder
White Oak	Red Maple	Tulip Poplar
Black Birch	Black Walnut	Butternut
Black Locust	Paper Birch	Quaking Aspen
Apple	Red Gum	Cottonwood
Blue Beech	Cherry	Willow
Crabs	Holly	Balsam Poplar
Red Oak	Grey Birch	
	Sycamore	
	Oregon Ash	
	Sassafras	
	Magnolia	

SOFTWOODS

High (Excellent)	Medium (Adequate)	Low (Fair)
Slash pine	Yew	Ponderosa Pine
Pond Pine	Tamarack	Red Fir
Western Larch	Nut pines—Pinyon	Noble Fir
Longleaf Pine	Shortleaf Pine	Black Spruce
	Junipers	Bald Cypress
	Loblolly Pine	Redwood
	Douglas Fir	Hemlocks
	Pitch Pine	Sitka Spruce
	Red Cedar	Yellow Cedar
	Norway Pine	White Spruce
		White Pine
		Balsam Fir
		Western Red Cedar
		Sugar Pine

For cooking, keep your fire small and hot. By placing a grill over the coals, you can soon have a substantial meal in the works. A large, blazing fire burns the food as well as the cook's hands.

Dutch-Oven Cooking—The Dutch oven is probably the most versatile piece of cooking equipment available to campers who enjoy cooking over an open fire. Because of its design and the cast iron it's made from, it distributes and holds heat evenly for a long period of time. It is ideal for shallow frying, deep-fat frying, stewing, baking, or roasting.

When hung by a hook over a fire, the Dutch oven can be used for boiling. If you place hot coals or glowing charcoal briquets under the Dutch oven and on its lid, you can use it for roasting and baking. And if you set the oven in the hot coals of a campfire or over several charcoal briquets, it can be used for stewing and frying.

I have been on many extended swamp trips where the Dutch oven was my entire cook kit. I found that the Dutch-oven lid, when turned upside down and placed on a small bed of hot coals, makes an excellent frying pan. If charcoal briquets are to be used, the pot can be turned upside down and 8 to 10 glowing briquets placed on the bottom. Then set the lid upside down on the oven's legs. This arrangement serves as an excellent camp griddle.

Two or more Dutch ovens can be stacked, with the hot coals on the lid of the lower oven heating the bottom of the upper oven, for baking several foods at one time.

In order to handle the hot ovens and to move hot coals, carry two tools with the Dutch oven. The first is a short-handled army-surplus shovel. This shovel is used for spreading coals, placing coals on the lid, and digging pits for cooking. The second tool is a short fireplace poker that is bent into a hook at the end. This tool allows you to move a hot oven, to lift a hot lid for checking food, and to move charcoal briquets around for proper spacing.

As with anything new, experience will help you master the skills of cooking in a Dutch oven.

Aluminum-Foil Cooking—Aluminum-foil cooking is far from new. Boy Scouts have been making campfire stews with foil for many years. I fondly recall my scouting days back in the early 1950s. Our favorite camp dessert was to take a banana, leaving the peel on, split it down the middle, and fill the split with caramel candy. Then we would wrap the banana with aluminum foil and toss it in a bed of coals. It was hard for us to wait those 10 minutes it took for the candy to melt into the hot banana.

Aluminum foil has many advantages for the camp cook. It gives you more time to hunt or fish since it reduces the time necessary for cleaning pots and pans down to zero. Foil cooking can reduce the number of pots you must take into the swamp. You can cook almost anything in foil, including vegetables, meats, and even fruit such as apples. Perhaps the thing I like best about foil cooking is that it is virtually foolproof.

When properly wrapped and sealed in foil, each bundle of food becomes a pressure cooker. The steam that is confined in the bundle retains flavor and prevents scorching. The only time food scorches is when steam escapes through a tear in the foil or when there's been a poor wrapping job.

Fish can be especially good when cooked in foil. Several years ago, I was on a week-long canoe trip down the Suwannee River. One afternoon we caught a few small "redbellied" sunfish. One of the old swampers on the trip taught me how to make a one-pot fish supper using foil. First he cleaned the sunfish. Then he spread about a tablespoon of margarine in the center of large sheets of aluminum foil. Two to three sunfish were placed on the foil. Next he spread margarine on the fish and sprinkled it with salt and pepper. On top of the fish he sliced potatoes and onions. His last ingredient was ketchup, with which he generously covered the vegetables and fish. He sealed the concoction in the foil bundles and placed them on hot coals, allowing them to cook on each side for 10 minutes. It was great! Each night after that we became redbellied-sunfish fishermen, hoping for another foil meal.

During a recent deer-hunting trip I made in the apple country of northwestern South Carolina, one of the local boys had his turn to cook, and we were giving him a hard time by demanding fresh apple pie. When we got into camp for dinner that night, we didn't have apple pie. But we did have some foil-cooked apples that were delicious. He had cored some fresh apples; filled the hole with cinnamon, sugar, and butter; and wrapped the apples in foil. He tossed them into a bed of coals for approximately 45 minutes, and we had a dish that was almost as good as apple pie.

Telling someone how long to cook an aluminum-foil dish is almost impossible. The best teacher is experience. In foil cooking, timing is not as critical as in other forms of cooking. You can usually learn without spoiling a meal.

When cooking in foil, be sure to place the food on the *shiny* side of the foil. Tests have proven that the shiny side of the foil reflects more radiant heat and causes less sticking.

There are two schools of thought about which works better—heavy-duty or lightweight foil. Camp cooks who use the heavy-duty foil say it is more desirable because of its additional strength. Cooks who use the lightweight foil usually wrap their food in two to three layers. They give three reasons for using the layer system and lightweight foil: (1) it is less likely to leak steam; (2) when they remove the bundle from the fire they take off the outer wrap, thereby getting rid of ashes; and (3) layers are less likely to break or tear than the single wrap. I've tried both weights of foil, and they both seem to work fine. So you be the judge.

Aluminum foil not only makes a good food wrap for campfire cooking but is also handy for making cooking utensils. Many backcountry travelers include foil in their survival kits. It should be in yours. Foil can be used for making a cup or a larger water container, pan, reflector oven, or skillet. Foil can also be used as an emergency signaling device. The reflective surface can be seen a long way on a bright day.

When you finish with your fire, drown it, stir it up, and drown it again. Soak not only your fire but also your rock ring if you used one, any logs that were in the fire, and the dirt under the fire. Never leave a fire unattended until you have thoroughly doused it. A little wind can bring a fire back to life unless it is thoroughly drowned. Don't be responsible for burning a precious swamp.

Before you leave the campsite, scatter the remains of your ashes so that no one will know you were there.

GARBAGE

The first lesson in camp sanitation is to keep several large plastic garbage bags and several smaller plastic garbage bags with your camp cooking gear. As you cook, put garbage in the bag. This habit keeps your camp clean and keeps pests away. Avoid cleaning fish and game in camp. Clean them well away from camp and put the waste parts in the smaller plastic bags, making sure you seal them tightly. At night and when you are away from camp, hang your garbage bag up high, in the same way you suspend your food-storage bag. You'll prevent some hungry critter from littering your camp. Fish guts pulled through camp by a raccoon can be a disappointing welcome back to camp.

There is no greater disappointment in the outdoor life than to spend hours getting back into a swamp and then find that some thoughtless camper has left behind his garbage. Bring out all your garbage. Burn all your food containers, and at the end you will find lots of aluminum foil in the ashes. Bring it out also. It will never disintegrate. Don't bury your garbage in a swamp. Since swamps are subject to flooding, the garbage may be washed out and deposited miles downstream. Or an animal will likely dig it up. Do your part to keep our swamps wild and beautiful. Always leave your campsite cleaner than you found it.

4

Water to Drink

Swamp camping takes you into an environment of readily available water, that is, it's readily available for everything except human consumption. Most swamps offer few, if any, sources of safe drinking water. I have traveled for days throughout the southern part of the nation with seasoned swamp guides and have observed their so-called secrets of finding "sweet water." In almost every case, they treated the clearer, running swamp water or they stopped by a trapper's cabin or farm and borrowed some safe water.

In order to enjoy your swamp hunting or fishing trip, you must understand the dangers of swamp water, where safe water may be found, and how to make swamp water safe to drink.

SWAMP-WATER DANGERS

There are basically three different types of swamps in this country: (1) the flood-plain swamp that is found along the sides of rivers, (2) the natural-depression swamp such as those formed by limesinks or other geological formations, and (3) the swamps caused by the damming of streams by beavers. Each of these swamp types has its own water problems.

The flood-plain swamp is fed by waters that originate upstream from runoff. Today most of our streams, especially in their lower reaches, are polluted with waste from cities, industries, agricultural areas, and even remote septic tanks. Regardless of how clear the flood-plain swamp water may look, *don't trust it*. Several years ago, two of my fishing pardners and I went deep into the Pascagoula River Swamp of Mississippi on a week-long search for bull bluegills. The running water next to our camp looked so clean that we didn't bother to treat it. It was a mistake that cut our trip short. We were weeks getting our stomachs back into proper working order.

The natural-depression swamp, in most areas, depends upon rainfall as its water source. Most of these swamps lack water movement, so they contain stagnant water that is subject to bacteriological contamination from animals. This is not always true of natural-depression swamps, the Okefenokee being one exception, but in most of these swamps the water is totally unfit for human consumption.

The beaver swamp is perhaps the only type of swamp that is growing in numbers today. Throughout much of this nation, especially in the South, the beaver population is on the increase. Many counties, which until recently had no beavers, are finding that much timber land is being converted into swamps by the activity of the new population of beavers. These swamps, while destroying many millions of dollars' worth of timber, are newfound hunting and fishing areas for the sportsman.

The water in these new beaver swamps have two major dangers. The first is from upstream pollution, as in flood-plain swamps. The beaver dam suddenly slows the water down and forms a collection basin for any upstream waste. The second danger, while found infrequently, is the disease tularemia. This disease is a very good reason for not drinking untreated beaver-swamp water. Water contaminated by the urine of beaver and other rodents has been known to transmit tularemia to man. Tularemia, sometimes known as rabbit fever, is a rare illness. But it can occur in beaver swamps.

FINDING SAFE WATER

The National Park Service states: "We know of no swamp waters that have met a safe-drinking-water test. It is only good judgment to purify the water, regardless of how pure it may look."

In my years of swamp living and traveling, I have found only two natural sources of safe drinking water.

The first source is the artesian wells found in many of the swamps in the South. Most of these ever-running fountains of fresh water are indicated on U.S. Geological Survey topographical maps. In my home state of Alabama, many of these wells along the Sipsey and Tombigbee River Swamps are continuously flowing through large pipes that stick 3 or 4 feet above the ground. These wells were discovered and piped by early settlers and plantation owners who had hoped to convert the swamps into agricultural lands. In the end, the swamps won, and now these piped fountains are a welcome relief to the swamp traveler. Artesian wells are also found along other southern river swamps and coastal swamps.

Sources of pure drinking water are extremely rare in swamps. At a few places, a pipe like this supplies pure water from an artesian well. But be sure before you drink.

The second natural source of safe water I've used is the water found in the interior of the Okefenokee Swamp. The Okefenokee is a natural-depression swamp, but it is higher than its border lands. Because of this unusual feature, the Okefenokee has no pollutants or contaminants washing in from outside. The swamp is fed by rainwater and to a great extent by clear, bubbling springs. Since the swamp is 130 feet above sea level, the water is in constant circulation. It drains away from a series of ridges in the center of the swamp into two distinct watersheds. As in most cypress swamps, the water of the Okefenokee is dark brown. This color is the effect of tannic acids from decaying vegetation, primarily cypress, and does not hurt the water quality. I have spent many days in this great swamp using the tea-colored water for drinking and cooking. I was always amused at the look on the faces of the city dwellers I was guiding when I dipped up a cup of the water and asked them if they wanted a drink. But the Okefenokee, like many of our wild areas, is changing because of increased visits by man. Now the manager of the Okefenokee Swamp suggests that the swamp water be treated.

MAKING SWAMP WATER SAFE TO DRINK

How can you be sure of having safe water? The first recommendation is obvious: carry enough treated water with you. This is great if you are traveling by truck, four-wheel-drive vehicle, or large boat. But what about such travel as backpacking or canoeing, where excess weight cannot be carried. Backpackers and canoeists who intend to travel in the swamp must learn how to treat water to make it safe for drinking.

Rule number one is: *never trust any water you are not absolutely sure of, no matter how crystal-clear the water may look.* Several years ago, while deer hunting in south Georgia, I was in a small creek swamp. Just to look at the sweet clear water made me thirsty. Because I was so intent on hunting, I resisted the urge to drink. Ten minutes upstream I waded around a sharp bend and buzzards flew in all directions. There, partly damming up my sweet clear water, was the carcass of a badly decomposed deer. Was I ever glad I hadn't tried that water!

Another caution before we talk about treatment. I have been told by many outdoorsmen that water running swiftly over rocks purifies itself. In fact, I know one fellow who swears that water is purified as it tumbles over the ninth rock. Don't you believe any of these claims. Water running over rocks may be aerated, but it's not purified. There's a mighty big difference.

Much of the water in swamps is off-colored. Sometimes this is caused by the vegetation, and other times it is caused by particles of dirt suspended in the water. According to the Alabama Department of Public Health, only clear water or water colored by tannic acid (as mentioned earlier) should be selected for treatment. Bacteria and viruses can be protected by particles of dirt. If clear water is unavailable, take the following steps with the water that is available: (1) filter the water through a clean handkerchief or similar fabric, (2) let the filtered water stand until any remaining sediment has settled to the bottom, (3) pour off the clear water into the vessel in which you plan to treat it, and (4) treat the water.

You should know several methods for treating questionable water.

The first is boiling. Boiling water for 10 minutes

almost guarantees germ-free water. Once the water has cooled, pour it back and forth several times between two containers to aerate it and thereby eliminate the flat taste that boiling gives it.

Over the years I have made it a habit to carry with me into the swamp a small backpack stove that operates on white gas. This lightweight but highly efficient stove can have water boiling in 5 minutes whether I'm camping on a platform in the middle of the Okefenokee Swamp or in a pirogue in southern Louisiana. It has given me hundreds of gallons of safe drinking water.

Another method of treating water is to use Clorox. That's right, the same Clorox you use for a brighter wash. To each quart of clear swamp water, add 10 drops of Clorox. If the water is cloudy, add 20 drops. Shake the water vigorously and then let it stand for 30 minutes. If there is a slight chlorine odor and taste, the water is adequately treated. If not, add another 10 drops and let the water stand for an additional 15 minutes. It may not taste great, but it's safe.

The iodine you may have in your first-aid kit also makes a good water treatment. Add 5 drops of iodine to 1 quart of clear water, 10 drops of iodine to 1 quart of cloudy water. Let it stand for 30 minutes, and drink up.

Today many commercial tablets are available at your drugstore for treating water. One of the old standbys is Halazone tablets. Two of these tablets added to a quart of water and followed by a 30-minute wait will do the trick.

Another tablet that is on the market is Potable Aqua. Found in most backpack shops, this potent tablet is packed in handy bottles of 50. One tablet will treat a quart of water.

Anytime you are treating water in a canteen or

This system, the Water Washer, is among the modern methods of purifying swamp water for drinking. Water is first treated with a chemical from the kit and then is poured through a filter that contains activated charcoal impregnated with silver.

container, be sure to splash some of the treated water on the cap, spout, lid, or other parts. You don't want to miss any germs that may come into contact with your mouth or water.

The new filtering devices now available containing silver and activated charcoal offer the swamp camper a modern method of water treatment. One that I have found to work well is the Water Washer Treatment Unit. Water is first treated with a chemical (part of the kit), and then it is poured through a filter containing activated charcoal impregnated with silver. Silver is a germ-killer. The unit is designed to purity 1,000 gallons before it needs a filter change.

Another water-treatment system is the ultra-light-weight one that's called Super Straw Pocket Water Washer. This effective little gadget, which looks like a fat straw and is made by American Water Purification, Inc., Pleasant Hill, California is a small (6 x ⅝ inch) water-treatment system that's ideal for backcountry travelers. It can treat 10 gallons of water, removing from it most agricultural pollutants, urban wastes, dirt, and sediments. Weighing less than an ounce, it is easy to stick in your pack or hunting coat.

With water treatments like these available, there is no excuse for having your good times in the swamp spoiled by foul drinking water. Think ahead. If your swamp trip takes you far from treated water, go prepared. Either take enough water with you, or take along one of these methods of treatment.

5

Canoe and Small-Boat Travel

One of the best outdoor adventures remaining in North America is to travel by boat or canoe deep into a swamp for hunting or fishing. The requirements for a trip of this type are relatively simple. Among them are: you must have the right type of craft for the intended trip, it must be loaded correctly, and you must know how to pick the best campsite. Other requirements such as trip planning, navigation, equipment, and so on are covered in other chapters of this book.

BOATS FOR SWAMPS

Watercraft for swamp travel are about as varied as the many swamps they're used in. Perhaps the most famous of all swamp boats is the Louisiana pirogue. This skinny, flat-bottomed, double-pointed boat was

The pirogue, a skinny, flat-bottomed, double-pointed craft, was the original swamp boat. It's for experts only—not for the occasional swamp visitor.

designed, out of necessity, by the swampers of Louisiana who actually lived out their lives in the bayous and swamps. The pirouge, though it's an excellent craft in skilled hands, is no craft for the occasional swamp visitor. So I won't cover its use in detail.

Many duck boats have been developed for use in shallow swamps, but they are not satisfactory for carrying camping gear.

Basically there are two types of watercraft that best serve the occasional swamp camper: (1) the johnboat, and (2) the canoe. Both of these craft work well in swamp rivers and in the standing, shallow swamps. Each, however, has its advantages under certain conditions. I have worked out a system over the years.

For running swamp rivers, I like a 12-foot-long johnboat. The most satisfactory rig I have ever owned for this purpose is the one I have now. It is a 12-foot 4-inch Grumman boat known as the 3.8. I have a 4.5-horsepower Mercury outboard motor with a remote

A fine rig for running swamp rivers is this 12-foot 4-inch Grumman boat known as the 3.8. The 4.5-horsepower Mercury moves it smartly, even with a load of camping gear.

tank. This motor pushes the little boat, even when loaded with a week's supply of camping gear, at a safe speed.

This rig works fine for running upstream to a hot fishing hole, carrying in the gear for a base camp for deer hunting, or guiding swamp visitors. This johnboat is made from aluminum, so I have practically no maintenance chores. In order to keep it quiet, I have put rubber car mats in the bottom so that tackle boxes and other gear will not bump and rattle. The 3.8 draws only 4 inches of water and is easy for me to slide over logs, sandbars, and other swamp-river obstacles.

For going back into the more typical shallow swamps, I prefer a canoe. Since a motor is almost impossible to use in many of these swamps, the canoe will get you through the lilies and between the trees with amazing speed. A few years ago, I started using the Sportspal ultralight canoe, and I've found it to be an ideal swamp craft. It is 14 feet long, made of aluminum, and weighs only 48 pounds. It's a delight to pull over stumps and logs. It is also quiet because its insides are padded with Ethafoam.

If you feel uneasy about using a canoe, sign up for a canoe class and pick up the necessary skill while having some fun. There are many canoeing classes held in the vicinity of most cities. On your first few swamp canoeing trips, try a rented canoe. Be sure you know what sort of canoe is best for you before you buy one. Most people find a canoe far less "tippy" and much easier to handle than they expected. For booklets on where to rent canoes and where canoe classes in your area are held, write to Grumman Boats. The address is listed in Chapter 18 under suppliers.

I don't mean to say that there aren't other equally

A canoe is the way to go back into shallow swamps where the use of a motor is impractical. This Sportspal 14-footer weighs only 48 pounds.

suited boats and canoes for swamp use. There are. But the two I've mentioned are the units I like and are cited only as examples of what you should look for in a swamp watercraft.

LOADING YOUR GEAR

Loading a watercraft for a swamp trip should be done with the same exactness as loading a canoe for white water. Many sportsmen are surprised to learn that some swamp-type rivers, especially during periods of low water, have sets of rapids. I'll never forget the surprise that Georgia swamp guide Jack McKey and I got once when running the swampy Alapaha River. We kept hearing what sounded like fast water around a bend. We couldn't believe it was rapids because we had run the river before and had found no fast water. For this reason, our gear was simply thrown in our canoe. As we rounded the bend, we saw that the low river narrowed to a chute between two rocks. It was too late. We were committed. The surprise caught us off guard, and soon we were swimming amid floating camping gear and Jack's dog.

In order to load your watercraft properly, follow these guidelines.

1. Place all your camping gear in waterproof bags (for details see Chapter 2 on equipment).

2. Place the bags in the boat or canoe about midway between the front and back. Shift the load around until it is balanced. In other words the craft, when loaded, should sit level in the water.

3. Be sure that the load does not crowd the occupants of the craft. Often in swamp travel you must get out of the craft to pull it over an obstacle or to break trail.

4. Tie your bags into the craft so that they can't shift. Tying also keeps them from being plucked out by low-hanging brush. And if your craft should capsize, your gear is still with the boat, not in the bottom of the swamp or downstream.

5. As a final check, you and your pardner get into the craft and see if the load is still balanced. Does the craft ride level in the water? If not, adjust the load.

Proper loading of your canoe or boat not only protects your gear but also makes your traveling safer and easier.

Properly done, the loading will get you over many obstacles with little or no effort. It will also help you make better time when traveling.

Make sure each occupant in your watercraft has a personal flotation device. Rope should be immediately available in the event the craft has to be pulled through shallow water. A machete also should be tied to the top of the load for possible trail-breaking or campsite clearing. An extra paddle is a must and should be easily reached.

CAMPSITE SELECTION

When traveling by watercraft in a swamp, campsite selection should be done by experience. If you don't know the area, get sound advice from someone who does know it and can tell you where possible campsites exist. I have made the mistake of going into an unfamiliar swamp and trusting to luck that by nightfall I would find a suitable campsite. Several times my luck ran out and those nights were long and uncomfortable. It is a helpless feeling to know that darkness is rapidly approaching and there's not a dry spot in sight.

Always plan your travel so that you are at your chosen campsite by midafternoon. Night comes early in the swamp, and you want plenty of light in which to set up your camp. If you think you can find the campsite after dark, you will probably discover that you are sadly mistaken. After dark, everything looks the same in the swamp. Landmarks have a way of disappearing.

When you pick a campsite, the first rule is to try for a dry one. Sometimes this is hard to do in the large interior of swamps. If you have a choice of a high site, take it. A little breeze will do a lot to keep mosquitoes away. If the site is weedy, cut down the weeds to open up the site. Openness discourages snakes and other pests. Always avoid the vicinity of dead trees, trees with dead tops, and leaning trees. Many times trees in swamps, especially on floating islands, are not firmly rooted. A night wind can bring them down on your camp.

When you travel on swamp rivers that have sandbars, you have the choice of some excellent campsites, provided you follow a couple of precautions. Be sure

If the river's not rising and the forecast doesn't call for rain, a sandbar campsite can be an excellent choice. Credit: Georgia Industry & Trade.

that the river is not rising, and be sure the weather forecast does not call for heavy rains. These sometimes snow-white sandbars are usually cool at night and are generally breezy enough to keep mosquitoes at a distance. The best tent for sandbar camping is a self-support pop tent.

An added advantage of a sandbar campsite is that you can fish right at camp. Also, you may see more wildlife. I have lain in my tent on several sandbar campsites and watched otter explore the camp area.

You can't normally walk out of a swamp, so carry a repair kit for your canoe or boat and motor. Be sure you've learned to use it before you head into the wilds. Credit: Georgia Industry & Trade.

One last caution about going down remote swamp rivers or deep into vast swamps. Know how to repair your boat, canoe, or outboard motor. Unlike many areas that sportsmen venture into, there's usually no walking out of the swamp. Carry a repair kit, and know how to use it. If you don't, you may have a long wait.

There is no question about it: seeing a swamp by watercraft is a real adventure. If you have a little experience and do some sound planning, swamp camping by boat or canoe can be the thrill of a lifetime.

6

Backpack Travel

Backpacking into swamps is an unfamiliar experience for most sportsmen. Until recently, it has been practiced by only a few hunters and explorers. But as more sportsmen turn to game-rich swamps to find uncrowded hunting and fishing, backpacking as a means of swamp travel is catching on fast.

In the Deep South, where swamps are the last real wilderness areas left, wild-turkey hunters are finding that by backpacking along old logging roads they can find old gobblers where there is little or no hunting pressure, and the camping is as much fun as the hunt. Ben Rodgers Lee, widely known wild-turkey caller and hunting guide, is convinced that many of the turkeys in deep river swamps never see a hunter during the spring season. Ben studies topographical maps of roadless areas in the swamps of Alabama's rivers. When he spots a likely area that's isolated from the roads, he gets the landowner's permission and backpacks in. As he proved to me several years ago, it's an excellent way to get your spring gobbler.

In principle, nothing is new about backpacking into

Though backpack trails are scarce in swamps and you may have to do considerable wading, more and more sportsmen are taking to the swamps with backpacks to find uncrowded fishing and hunting.

swamps. The Indians perfected the art hundreds of years ago. They taught it to the explorers and settlers of the 1700s.

What *is* new about swamp backpacking is the equipment. Modern science has given us new lightweight backpacking systems that allow us, even those who are not supermen, to enjoy packing our camp comfortably into an uncrowded swamp.

THE PACK

As a backpacker, you're something like the swamp turtle: you carry your home on your back. So the first item of equipment is the packframe and bag. Today's frames are made of lightweight aluminum or plastic. You will want to get one that has padded shoulder straps and a padded hip belt. The padded hip belt is a tremendous improvement on packframes. The old-fashioned frames made you carry the weight on your shoulders, and you were constantly off balance. The hip belt transfers much of the pack's weight from the shoulders and spine to the much stronger hips and legs, thus allowing you to move about naturally. Good balance is especially important when you will be doing a lot of wading. For several years I have used a Camp Trails packframe with much satisfaction. Next I tried the Blue Ridge III backpack made by Diamond Brands of Naples, North Carolina. It is an excellent backpack that has exceeded all my expectations.

Many deer hunters in the Great Lakes States and New England States have discovered backpacking as a way of getting into trophy-deer areas in dense swamps. Bringing a big buck out one quarter at a time can be hard work, but the rewards are well worth it.

Backpack hunting shouldn't have to be a long drive from home. Many nearby swamps are overlooked as good game habitat. I know a Georgia deer hunter who backpacks into the large clear-cuts on the land of a pulp and paper company near his home. Then he hunts the pockets of swamp that the woodcutters couldn't get into. He packs out a good buck, a quarter at a time, every year. Another friend of mine over in Arkansas takes his two young sons each fall on a couple of backpack trips into a local river swamp for squirrels. He says it is the high point of the year for him and his boys.

Some of the best fishing in the country is found in beaver swamps and creek swamps that are overlooked by most fishermen. I have found some excellent trout fishing by packing into various miniature swamps that beaver have made in the Appalachian Mountains.

I make it a point to carry an ultralight spinning outfit with me anytime I backpack into a swamp. One of the few bluegills I've ever caught that weighed over 2 pounds was landed on such a trip. And recently while backpacking for wild turkey, I found several holes in a creek swamp that gave me so much largemouth action I almost quit chasing gobblers to spend all my time fishing.

The bag that fits on your packframe is where all your camping gear is stored, so it must be of the highest quality. The swamp is no place to have a torn pack bag. A quality bag will be made from the strongest water-proof coated-nylon material. The thread will be either nylon or rotproof cotton-wrapped polyester. The quality bag will have heavy-duty zippers. I have found it a good idea to tie a stout cord through each zipper's slide so that the zippers can be easily opened during cold weather without taking off my gloves.

Most quality bags will have at least seven compart-

ments or pockets in which to pack your camping gear—
two on each side of the bag, one on the outside flap,
and two large compartments on the inside main part of
the bag. Of the two large compartments, the upper one
is covered by the bag flap and the lower one can be
opened without removing the flap.

It is the organization of your gear in these seven
compartments that makes setting up camp fast and
easy. And proper organization keeps items you will
need on the trail close at hand and not buried so that
you must unpack to find them. It is very unsatisfying to
have to unload a backpack just to get a drink of water.

In my many years of living out of a backpack, I have
developed a packing system that works very well for
me. Here it is:

The two upper side pockets each contain one plastic
canteen of water. These are easy to reach while walking
in a swamp without unpacking anything. Someone with
me can reach a canteen even while the pack remains on
my back.

The outside pocket on the flap is where I keep my
topo maps and fishing and hunting license in a waterproof container. I refer to my maps regularly, and this
pocket is easy to get to. The quality bag will also have
leather lashing patches for tying on fishing rods, wading boots, and such.

The four other pockets of the bag I think of as a
house. They are my bathroom, kitchen, and bedroom.
The two lower side pockets are the bathroom.

The pocket on the lower left contains a toothbrush,
toothpaste, soap (hotel size), and toilet paper carefully
sealed in a zip-loc plastic bag. Wet toilet paper is no fun
in a swamp. The last item in this pocket (kept on top) is
a Mallory Duracell compact flashlight. Many times I
have packed in on a late Friday afternoon after work

Here's how the author arranges gear in his backpack

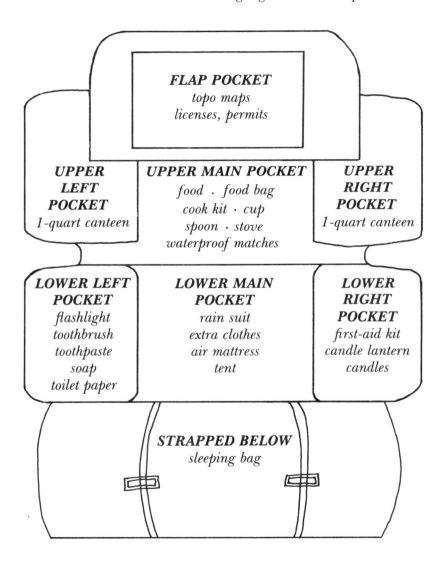

FLAP POCKET
*topo maps
licenses, permits*

**UPPER
LEFT
POCKET**
1-quart canteen

UPPER MAIN POCKET
*food . food bag
cook kit · cup
spoon · stove
waterproof matches*

**UPPER
RIGHT
POCKET**
1-quart canteen

**LOWER LEFT
POCKET**
*flashlight
toothbrush
toothpaste
soap
toilet paper*

**LOWER MAIN
POCKET**
*rain suit
extra clothes
air mattress
tent*

**LOWER
RIGHT
POCKET**
*first-aid kit
candle lantern
candles*

STRAPPED BELOW
sleeping bag

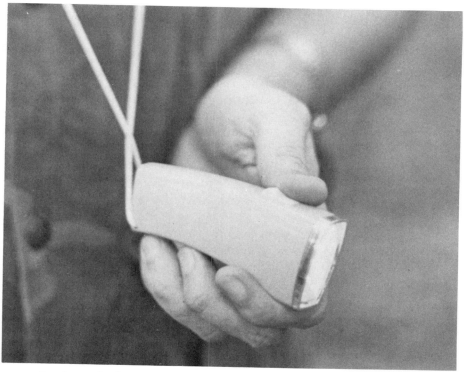

In the author's system of packing, his compact flashlight is kept at the top of one pocket of his backpack for instant availability. It comes in handy for setting up camp after dark.

and had to set up camp in the dark. That flashlight had to be easy to find.

In the lower right pocket, I keep a small first-aid kit, including water-purification tablets. In this pocket I also carry a folding candle lantern with two types of candles. The stearic-acid plumber's candle burns slowly, hotly, and with a bright flame. Most important, it won't melt in the heat of my pack as a paraffin candle will. I also carry a supply of citronella candles to burn in my lantern if the mosquitoes are swarming. These candles do a good job keeping the flying pests at a distance. Furthermore, candles are good fire-starters. And melted candle wax rubbed into the fabric will stop a minor tent leak. Also, candle wax rubbed onto pack or sleeping-bag zippers makes the zipping much easier.

The upper big pocket in the bag is my kitchen. Here I keep freeze-dried food, small cook kit, plastic cup, spoon, backpack stove, matches in a waterproof container, and a waterproof bag in which to hang the food in a tree to prevent raccoons, skunks, and bears from stealing my supper.

The lower big pocket is my bedroom. Here I carry my two-man backpack tent, air mattress, extra clothes, and rain suit. The rain suit is on top and easy to reach in a hurry.

Under the bag, strapped securely to the packframe, I carry my sleeping bag packed in a waterproof stuff bag.

THE TENT

Perhaps the most important part of any overnight swamp trip is the ability to sleep comfortably. A good night's rest will help make you a better hunter or fisherman. It will also make those early-morning risings much easier. The first component to sleeping well is a good tent. I have slept in brush lean-tos, in a blanket under the stars, in snow caves, and in various other makeshift shelters. And I have been eaten alive by mosquitoes, rained on, kept awake by the cold, and had a copperhead sleep next to me. In short, nothing takes the place of a good tent. A modern backpack tent usually is made of flame-resistant, coated ripstop nylon. The right tent has a sewn-in waterproof floor, storm flaps, and insect netting on doors and vents. Swamp backpackers particularly like two qualities about these little tents: (1) set-up time is less than 10 minutes, and (2) weight is only around 6 pounds.

One spring I went on a backpack fishing trip with John Phillips, the noted swamp fisherman. John and I used a Camel Deluxe Teton lightweight tent, and we were pleased with its performance. It kept the south Alabama mosquitoes on the outside, and we had enough room on the inside.

Another new rig I am using is the Coleman Peak 1 tent. It is a high-quality tent that sets up in 5 minutes and has passed all tests as an excellent backpack tent. There are many good backpack tents on the market,

In backpack camping, nothing takes the place of a good tent. This Peak 1 model passes all tests as an excellent backpack tent. Credit: Coleman Co.

but there are also many "cheapies" that are designed to sell, not use. When you shop for a backpack tent, stick to reputable brands and see one get put up and taken down before you decide to buy.

Since most of your swamp backpack camps may be on wet or damp ground, carry a piece of heavy-duty plastic that's cut an inch smaller all around than the tent floor. Set your tent up over this ground cover for a drier tent floor.

THE SLEEPING BAG AND MATTRESS

The next step to a comfortable night is a soft spot to sleep on. I have read of hardy outdoorsmen who just slept on the ground, but I find very few who actually do it. Many of today's youthful backpackers sleep on polyethylene pads. Others sleep on short foam pads that cushion only from head to hips. My preference is to lay my old bones on a full-length air mattress, complete with pillow. I'll admit that it's heavier (5 pounds) than other choices, and I must huff and puff to get it inflated. But it's worth the effort after a hard day in the swamp.

The backpacker's sleeping bag should be of the mummy shape, a style that offers warmth without excessive weight. The amount and type of insulation in the sleeping bag is the primary element in keeping you warm. The three best-known insulating fillers for sleeping bags are: down, Dac II, and Polar-Guard. Each has its good points and weak points. Down loses its insulating qualities when it gets wet; the two others don't. Down and Dac II will leak out of a torn bag; Polar-Guard won't. Polar-Guard will not compact well for packing; down and Dac II will. Confusing? You bet.

After many years of trying them all, I have settled on a bag filled with 3 pounds of Polar-Guard for swamp camping conditions. I carry the sleeping bag in a tough, waterproof ripstop-nylon stuff sack on my pack to guard against its getting torn. The choice is yours, but be sure you get a reliable brand and not a bargain-basement sleeping bag. The brand-name sleeping bag may cost more, but it will more than pay for the extra expense in many nights of comfortable sleep.

FOOD

Not too many years ago, backpack foods were practically all dehydrated, and each soggy meal was about as appealing as the powdered eggs so many of us ate in the armed forces. Well, I'm pleased to report that this has all changed. Through the process known as freeze-drying, food companies such as Mountain House, Rich-Moor, and Chuck Wagon (to name just a few) have come up with many delicious dishes that are precooked, premeasured, and simply require boiling water to prepare. Dishes such as pork chops, sausages, shrimp creole, spaghetti and meatballs, chicken stew, beef stroganoff, and almost any vegetable are available to the backpacker.

Modern backpack meals are nutritious, lightweight, and easy to prepare. If you can boil water, you can eat food. They're fairly expensive, but I consider them worth the price.

STOVES

Not so long ago it would take an hour or more when we returned to our camp to get a fire going and prepare a meal. With today's backpack food and a highly efficient little backpack stove, a full meal can be prepared from start to serving in about 10 minutes. Most of the backpack stoves weigh somewhere between 2 and 4 pounds and will boil water in 5 to 15 minutes. During a recent backpack trip I took with outdoor writer Tom Gresham, he and I had a cooking race to compare my LP gas stove's water-boiling time against that of Tom's new Peak 1 Coleman stove, which uses white gas. At the end of 10 minutes, Tom was serving dinner while I was just dropping my beef stroganoff into my barely boiling water. The following week I ordered one of the new Coleman stoves.

With the help of whatever backpack stove you choose, if it's a good one, you can be eating a hot meal within 20 minutes after you get into camp. I also know outdoorsmen who use these little stoves for making coffee on the front decks of their swamp boats and, of all places, in their deer-hunting tree stands.

BOOTS

Sometimes it seems as if there are about as many different kinds of hiking boots as there are backpackers. My choices of boots for drier swamp walking are the Browning Hi-Land Featherweights with the semicleat sole and the Sears lightweight sport boot with the lug sole. These boots should be coated with Sno-Seal between swamp trips. For walking in moist-to-wet areas, the L. L. Bean rubber-bottom leather-top boot is hard to beat. If I am going into an area during warm weather that requires some wading, I usually wear a pair of G.I. Jungle Boots and carry a pair of moccasins to wear around camp. When I don't need to be concerned about the weight, I take along a spare pair of boots.

Perhaps the main point that should be stressed about backpack footgear is that you wear a comfortable boot that is well broken in. A backpack trip is no place for hurting feet.

Also remember to dry your wet boots slowly. I have seen many swamp campers set their boots next to a campfire to rush the drying process and end up with hard, brittle boots.

FISHING TACKLE

It is not the purpose of this book to teach you how to fish. But backpack camping does require certain differences in tackle, so I feel it's necessary to at least discuss a few basics.

Every ounce must be carefully considered, and so must the length of rods and their safe carrying. Within these limitations, the backpack fisherman has two basic systems of fishing gear to select from. The first is a new ultralight spinning outfit that breaks down to fit into a backpack or can be easily tied on. From among the many good ones available, I have chosen the Dalwa Minicast-Gold closed-face spinning outfit. It has a 5-foot rod that breaks down into five short pieces, and total weight of rod and reel is only 20 ounces. The rod and reel pack neatly into a plastic carrying case that is only 15 inches long.

The second system is designed for fishermen who

like to use both a flyrod and spinning rod or for fishermen who want to use tackle heavier than ultra-light. This system uses a longer, heavier combination rod and a medium-weight fly or spinning reel. The outfit of this type that I've used with satisfaction is the Eagle Claw Trailmaster six-piece rod. When it's put together, it's 6 feet 9 inches long. I have found that any medium-weight fly reel or open-face spinning reel will work well on this compact rod. It comes in a 15-inch aluminum tube that makes packing it easy.

As for carrying your lures, spinners, flies, and other tackle, select one of the little tackle boxes such as those made by Umco. Carefully select a few of the best lures for the species of fish you want to catch. You won't be able to carry nearly as much tackle as you usually carry, but you'll be surprised after a trip or two just how little tackle you really need.

TRAIL SELECTION

For many years, most of the backpacking-trail development in the United States was restricted to the mountains. Within recent years, however, trail planners have started developing trails into other environments, including swamps. In fact, Florida now has several hundred miles of trail, much of which goes through some of the most beautiful swamps in the country. Though the development of trails into swamps is under way, most of the areas of interest to sportsmen are still without a formal trail system.

The best way to overcome this obstacle is to use a U.S. Geological Survey topographical map. Within the past 100 years, most of our swamps have been logged by timber companies. In order to harvest the trees and haul the logs out, the swamps have been penetrated by logging roads and narrow-gauge railroads. The topographical maps show these logging roads and railroad beds. Since these were built along the driest routes (and in some cases built up above the flood level) they make excellent hiking trails.

When no trail or old roadbed is available, you should approach swamp backpacking with caution. Under ideal conditions, walking into and back out of a large swamp requires not only advanced wilderness navigational skills but also some advance knowledge of the area. Spend some time with the local residents before trying such a feat. I have spent 2 days trying to backtrack out of a swamp that it took me only 1 day to get into. Had I talked to the local people, I would have found out that the area I was trying to reach was impossible to reach by walking. Instead of spending an enjoyable weekend of camping and fishing, I spent a weekend trying to get out of a waist-deep "green hell." Plan your trips carefully and you will find that swamp backpacking is as much fun as mountain backpacking, with a little more sense of adventure thrown in.

CAMPSITE SELECTION

The selection of a good campsite in a swamp environment is a combination of research; planning; and, to some degree, luck. You will need to find out beforehand whether any new swamp you plan on going into is suitable for backpacking. Ask the people you check with if they know of suitable campsites. To know of good campsites ahead of time is a definite advantage.

Planning is a major part of campsite selection, especially when you'll walk miles into a swamp. With a boat, canoe, or motor vehicle you can, if necessary, camp with reasonable comfort almost anywhere. But when you're on foot, you must find a campsite before you can unroll your sleeping bag.

If you ignore research and planning, you'll need a lot of luck to camp comfortably. Swamps are mostly flat, so they appear on U.S. Geological Survey topographical maps as a vast green area with swamp symbols covering it. There is little evidence to give you any clue to good campsites. Even under the best of conditions, dry suitable campsites are scarce in most swamps. Some luck is necessary anytime you are traveling from one site to another on foot.

The first rule of campsite selection for the swamp backpacker is to start looking for a suitable spot early in the afternoon. Darkness has a way of coming early and swiftly in the dense vegetation. To wait until late afternoon for campsite selection is a mistake you won't want to make often.

Another reason I like to make camp early, especially during the warm months, is to get all the camp chores done and supper eaten before dark. This schedule permits me to get into my tent early to escape the mosquitoes that darkness brings. When morning comes, I've had a good night's sleep and am ready at daybreak for hunting or fishing.

Once you have decided to call it a day on the trail and make camp, start looking for an open, dry area. Open in a swamp means an area free of underbrush, blow-downs, and such. Air should circulate—a must for relief from mosquitoes. On occasions I have known it to be necessary to cut underbrush in order to create an open campsite. Some looking, however, will usually enable you to avoid the brush cutting.

Once you have located a dry, open area, check the

nearby trees. Are they the tallest around? If so, they may attract lightning. Are any of these trees dead (a common scene in many swamps) or do they have dead limbs? If so, a sudden wind could put you in danger of being hit by a falling tree or limb.

Not long ago, I was guiding Phil Chase, public-relations director of the Connecticut Valley Arms Company, in an Alabama swamp when a windstorm caught us out in an area where many of the trees had dead limbs. Suddenly we were being showered by chunks of wood. It didn't take us long to get into a safer area. Be observant. Know what's over your campsite, and don't take unnecessary risks.

As for finding a dry campsite, there are several "rules of thumb" you can follow. If you're hiking an old logging road or railroad bed as a trail, it's a good idea to use the roadbed as a campsite. They're not always dry, but throughout the country I've found good campsites along most swamp roadbeds that I've gone in on. If you're in an area where pine trees grow, especially in the South, they are usually a good indicator of dry land. They die if they stand in water very long.

Another trick I picked up in Missouri from an old swamp trapper is that if you are using an older U.S. Geological Survey topographical map, it may show houses, small swamp farms, and so on that have been long vacated and torn down. These pioneers didn't live in water, and their homesites make excellent campsites. Several times I have found good water still available at these forgotten homesteads. One of my favorite swamp backpack campsites for squirrel hunting is the site of a turn-of-the-century sawmill. I didn't see it on a map. A local landowner told me about it. The old site is on a little rise in the swamp, and a vehicle can't get within 5 miles of it. I've been hunting into this remote, heavily wooded campsite many times and have never seen another hunter.

Finding a swamp campsite for backpacking is a challenge. With some experience, however, you'll acquire a skill that any sportsman would be proud to have.

HOW TO GET STARTED

Perhaps the best way to break into swamp backpacking is to visit your local backpack shop. Rent a complete outfit, and go on a short overnight trip with an experienced backpacker. Learn what equipment best suits your needs, and then buy gear made by reputable manufacturers. Next, start exploring where you can escape the crowds. The search for overlooked swamps and the study of topo maps can be fun in themselves. When hunting or fishing season rolls around invite a close friend, son, daughter, or wife to join you. Put your home on your back, and hike into a swamp. Within a few minutes' walking time, you'll find yourself in an outdoor setting that most other people never see. Whether or not you take your bag or creel limit, your trip will be an adventure you will remember. Suddenly you will wonder why you had never backpacked into a swamp before.

7

Four-Wheel-Drive-Vehicle Travel

Many swamps have logging roads on their edge, and a few even have logging roads into their interior. To the sportsman who owns a four-wheel-drive (4 WD) vehicle, these logging roads are trails to adventure. The four-wheeler can carry plenty of camping gear plus a boat, and still get you to your campsite quicker than any other means of swamp travel. That's the good news. The bad news is that the four-wheel-drive vehicle might get stuck.

STAYING UNSTUCK

My work in wildlife management brings me into contact each year with hundreds of sportsmen who are using four-wheel-drive vehicles to get into swamps. Most of these people are experienced campers but are

With a four-wheel-drive vehicle, you can travel by logging road into parts of some swamps and carry a boat or canoe and plenty of gear.

obviously somewhat inexperienced in driving through the mud and sand found in and around swamps. I see scores of these vehicles stuck, and most could have avoided the problem.

A lot of new owners of four-wheelers—and there are thousands every year now—think just because they paid $10,000 for their vehicle and it has big tires, plus a winch, that it can swim through the deepest mud hole. This attitude can only lead to trouble.

Let's start from the beginning and see how the driver

of a four-wheel-drive vehicle should approach swamp driving.

First of all, you should have permission from the landowner to use the logging roads and to camp. Much of the land in and around swamps belongs to private companies or individuals. It is only right that you should get their permission before using their property.

Next, get your vehicle ready for the trip. Proper tires should have round shoulders and a moderately aggressive tread such as the standard mud-grip tread. You should have a power winch installed if your budget can stand the cost. You should also have a tool chest that includes snow chains (even though you don't expect snow), shovel, ax, hand-operated tire pump, two jacks, 50-foot nylon tow strap (10,000-pound test), two 2-inch-thick by 1-foot-wide by 2-foot-long planks, and a set of wrenches.

If you don't have a winch, be sure and add what's known as a "come-along" to your tool chest. The come-along is simply a hand-powered winch. It is best described as a hand-cranked, cable-filled wheel and ratchet. You attach one end of the cable to a tree and the come-along to the vehicle frame. Each time you pump the handle, the wheel takes up the cable, winching you out of the mud hole.

With this assortment of emergency gear, you are ready to load up your camping equipment and head for the swamp.

Once you leave maintained roads, the trick is to travel slowly and study the road carefully. If there is any doubt about the condition of the road ahead, stop, get out of your vehicle, and do a little walking. How deep is the mud, or how deep is the hole under the water? Use a stick, and test each situation. Common sense should tell you when to turn around and find a new route.

If the going looks as though it's going to get rough, put on your tire chains. They work as well in slick mud as they do in snow. Another trick to use, especially in deep sand, is to decrease your tire pressure to approximately 12 pounds. This allows your tires to "float." Don't forget to inflate them again as you get out of the trouble area.

Learn to use your winch (or your come-along) before you actually need it. Numerous times I have come upon a shiny new four-wheel-drive vehicle stuck and found the owner trying to figure out how to use his winch. When you buy your winch, make sure the salesman gives you a good session in its proper use.

The most frustrating situation, and one of the most common, that swamp four-wheelers find themselves in is to have all four wheels stuck—unable to move forward or backward. If you have an electric winch, the solution is to hook the cable to a tree and throw the switch. If you don't have a winch, then hook up your come-along and sweat a little. Use your shovel to clear the way for each tire to move. If you don't have either of these devices, a third possibility is to get an accompanying vehicle to pull you out.

If you have none of these options, you are in for some work. You must shovel away all the mud that's piled up underneath the vehicle. This is supporting the weight of the chassis and keeping weight off the tires, thereby causing the tires to lose traction.

Once you have the vehicle's under-carriage free of mud, get out a jack and plank. Using the plank as a platform for the jack, raise the wheel that is deepest in the mud. Dig out the mud beneath the wheel down to a firm base. Then fill up the hole with rocks, logs, brush, and such. Now lower the wheel slowly down onto the firm platform you've constructed. Do the same thing to each of the other wheels. Then extend the solid platforms for several feet in front of each wheel. If you don't, you'll be able to move forward only a few feet and then will be back into the same predicament.

Sandy areas around the edge of swamps should be traveled over with caution. Ford Motor Company advises that the important thing to remember in sand or soft dirt is to keep moving steadily and not too fast. Don't apply an excess of power that would cause the wheels to dig in. Try to avoid abrupt changes in speed or direction, and aim as straight as possible across the area. Avoid sharp turns. Sharp turns cause the front tires to scrub sideways, turning them into plows that can raise impassable pileups of the sand. (A booklet entitled "A Close Look At 4-Wheel Driving" covers most stuck situations and is available free by writing to Ford Motor Company, P.O. Box 1978, Dearborn, Michigan 48121.)

It would take a book to list the various ways people get stuck in swamps with their vehicles and the ways to get them out. If only they would learn the capabilities and limits of their vehicles and how to read swamp roads, most of these situations would be avoided. Unavoidable pitfalls can be remedied in a short time by knowing how to use your emergency equipment and applying it with a little common sense.

CAMPSITE SELECTION

Campsite selection is not as critical for the four-wheeler as it is for the backpacker or boating camper. The four-wheeler can cover long distances in a fraction of the time it takes the other types of campers to cover a mile or two. If the four-wheeler gets caught by dark or storms, he can spend the night in his vehicle with reasonable comfort.

Around many of the larger swamps are a fair number of public and private campgrounds. The vehicle-traveling camper can look them up in one of the popular campground directories.

For more remote campsites, the four-wheeler can check with the owner of the land on which he will travel. Many times the forester with a pulp-and-paper company, the biologist with a wildlife refuge, or the local owner will know of choice hidden campsites that you can reach with your vehicle.

Another enjoyable way to find campsites that can be reached by four-wheel-drive vehicles is to acquire maps of the swamp and its surrounding area. Study the road system, especially roads that lead directly into the swamp. I have done this many times and discovered some excellent campsites at old sawmill sites, homesteads, and one time at an old fort. By following these roads and being friendly, you will meet some of the most interesting people. In fact, many times I've been invited to share a hunt or a fishing hole with these backcountry citizens. They also know the campsites with clean water and are always good for a story or two.

If you decide to take your four-wheel-drive vehicle miles back into the swamp, learn something about the

In and around some swamp areas, it's even possible for a four-wheel-drive rig to tow a lightweight camper such as this folding model.

road beforehand. Many times a dry road of gumbo clay becomes impassable after rain. And a weather check is always in order during hunting season. A sudden snowstorm can put you to unexpected homesteading for several days.

FOUR-WHEEL-DRIVE-VEHICLE ETIQUETTE

At this writing, there is a movement to restrict the use of four-wheel-drive vehicles in many backcountry areas, including swamps. The dissatisfaction arises out of overuse and abuse of some natural areas. If four-wheel-drive vehicles are to remain a means of backcountry travel, the following rules of etiquette are a must for all four-wheelers.

1. Get permission before entering anyone's land.
2. Leave all gates the way you found them.
3. Bring your garbage out with you.
4. Leave your campsite as though no one was ever there.
5. Be courteous to everybody you meet.
6. Do not stray off roads on to planted trees, pastures, and crops.
7. Obey hunting and fishing laws.
8. Report violations.
9. Do not tear up roads by overuse. If a road is extremely muddy, stay off until it dries thoroughly.
10. Avoid leaving deep tire tracks that turn into gullies.

8

Safety and First Aid

This chapter is not designed to make you a Red Cross first-aid instructor nor is it designed to take the place of the Red Cross First-Aid Manual. I recommend that you take the Red Cross First-Aid Course before you venture into any outdoor setting. This chapter deals with the dangers, both real and to some degree imaginary, of the swamp environment. I hope that when you finish reading this chapter you will have a better understanding of the real swamp dangers, and you will know the facts about some of the imaginary swamp dangers.

SNAKES

Several years ago while guiding for Wilderness Camping and Guide Service in south Georgia, I noticed that many clients cancelled swamp trips because of their fear of snakes. They believed that all swamps were full of slithering, poisonous serpents waiting to feed on anybody who dares enter their watery domain. Clients who did take the trips were always surprised to see how few snakes we actually encountered. In fact, many clients acted as though they were cheated if we didn't see a cottonmouth or diamondback rattlesnake.

Although the snake danger in swamps is highly overrated, especially in the northern half of the nation, there is still a need for swamp campers to understand snake danger and what to do in the unlikely event of snakebite.

It has been estimated that some 8,000 people in the United States are bitten by poisonous snakes each year. Of these, only about 12 die. However, many of the others endure long periods of suffering and either lose limbs or end up with deformities. For the swamp camper, it is somewhat comforting to note that only 8 percent of the total number of snakebites occur near water.

The poisonous snakes that should be of interest to the swamp camper are the cottonmouth, the massasauga rattlesnake, the copperhead, the eastern diamondback rattlesnake, and the canebreak rattlesnake.

Cottonmouth—The overrated reputation of the cottonmouth has probably kept more sportsmen out of southern swamps than has any other reason. Commonly called water moccasin, the cottonmouth has received much more than its share of negative publicity around campfires.

The color pattern of the cottonmouth is dull and inconspicuous: dark-brown bars on a somewhat lighter background. Many cottonmouths look either dirty brown or uniform black. I have seen some that were difficult to identify because of variance in their color patterns. The most positive identification is the elliptical

The cottonmouth is sometimes difficult to identify because of variations in the color pattern. Most positive identification feature is the elliptical vertical pupil of the eye. Credit: U.S. Fish & Wildlife Service.

vertical pupil of the eye. The cottonmouths get their name from their habit of threatening an intruder with open mouth, revealing a cotton-white interior.

Although some individual cottonmouths exceed 5 feet in length, most are from 3 to 4 feet long. Occasionally these snakes will grow to an alarming size. At this writing there is a live cottonmouth on display at the Okefenokee Swamp Park near Waycross, Georgia, that is 4 feet 3 inches in length and weighs 9 pounds. Only twice in all my years of swamp camping have I ever seen wild cottonmouths this large.

The cottonmouth range is much smaller than most people believe. I have heard the cry "cottonmouth" from Vermont to Kansas, but the range is much smaller. Generally their range runs south of a line from south-central Texas up through the Mississippi River Basin in Missouri, down along the Tennessee River Basin, and up the east coast through Virginia. The cottonmouth is most commonly found in areas where the elevation is below 800 feet. More often than not, supposed cottonmouths turn out to be various non-poisonous watersnakes that belong to the natrix family. These snakes are aggressive, and some do resemble the cottonmouth, but they are not poisonous.

Though the cottonmouth is much scarcer than many swamp visitors believe, when he is found he should be avoided. He is curious and is no coward. The cotton-mouth is slow to retreat. Many times I have seen one hold its ground when escape would have been easy.

The cottonmouth's apparent curiosity never ceases to amaze me. Several years ago while managing a wild-hog hunt in a large swamp near Valdosta, Georgia, I was sitting at the checking station and talking with a group of at least a dozen hunters. Suddenly a large cotton-mouth crawled into our midst as though he had been invited. That bull session ended fast.

On another occasion, I was with my good friend Don Pfitzer of the U.S. Fish and Wildlife Service and a group of outdoor writers on a tour of the Okefenokee Swamp. As we walked along a boardwalk out into the swamp, we saw two large cottonmouths on the swamp floor next to the boardwalk. As the group watched and took pictures, the two cottonmouths went on with their mating, unafraid of our group.

The best prevention against a cottonmouth bite is precaution. When you're in cottonmouth territory, keep your eyes open and always watch where you place your feet and hands. When you travel in a boat, watch overhanging limbs, stumps, logs, and the base of trees. Cottonmouths like to sun themselves, as other water snakes do. Several times I have almost grabbed a snake by reaching around a tree to tie up a boat. Look before you put your hands anywhere.

Another place you are likely to encounter a cottonmouth is on the end of your fish stringer. There is not a more sobering experience than to pull up a stringer of fish and find a big cottonmouth attached, swallowing one of the fish. That hazard is a good argument for carrying an ice chest to keep your catch.

I have never known anyone who has had a cottonmouth come into camp, but I have had a rattlesnake and copperhead pay a visit. For this reason, I advocate a clean campsite. If you are forced to choose a weedy campsite, take the time to trim the weeds down all around the entire area. Keep alert while you do it. Also keep your gear off the ground and stored neatly. If you must move around at night, do so only with a light. Examine each step before you take it. A clean, well-organized camp will usually discourage crawling visitors. But if they do decide to visit, a little caution will enable you to see them first.

It is a common practice among campers to turn a boat or canoe over at the end of the day. For some unknown reason, an overturned boat becomes a favorite resting site for a cottonmouth. So turn boats upright cautiously, and make sure you don't have a stowaway coiled under a bow or seat. Once you have shoved off into the swamp is a heck of a time to realize that you have a snake for a passenger.

I have heard stories of cottonmouths that dropped into boats or tried to get into boats. But I have never known any reliable swamp traveler who has actually had such an experience. I have also heard that a light in a swamp attracts cottonmouths. Again, I don't know of any actual cases, and in my several hundred nights spent in swamps, I've never seen it happen.

All water snakes, however, do seem to be curious. They do swim around boats. Your light will occasionally spot one during a session of frog-gigging or night fishing. But I doubt that you will ever be attacked. After spending half of my life in swamps, I have known of only a dozen people who were bitten by cottonmouths. Half of these people didn't look where they placed their feet or hands. The other half were "snake experts" who were bitten while catching cottonmouths.

Massasauga Rattlesnake—Most of the poisonous snakes found in swamps are indigenous to the South, but the massasauga rattlesnake (or swamp rattler, as he is commonly called) is not a southerner. His range runs from south Texas across the Midwest into the Great Lakes states. This small rattlesnake, usually 2 to 3½ feet in length, is mild tempered and does not strike unless he has been very much annoyed or is in search of food. The color of the massasauga rattlesnake is ashy gray, with large, irregularly rounded black blotches on his back.

This little rattlesnake is found around the edges of swamps and bogs. Caution should be used especially in erecting camp and walking around camp. Its small size makes it less dangerous than the larger poisonous snakes, but the massasauga is not to be taken lightly. It's difficult to see, and once I almost picked up one while gathering firewood.

Copperhead—The copperhead is often thought of as a high-country snake that prefers mountains and rocky areas. Such habits may be somewhat true of the northern copperhead, but its southern brother is mainly a snake of the lowlands, of low ground near swamps and swamp streams. Copperheads are found throughout most of the eastern half of the United States and in the lower midwestern states. The southern copperhead is found in the swamp areas of North Carolina, South Carolina, Georgia, Alabama, Mississippi, Louisiana, Missouri, Arkansas, and Texas.

One problem most campers have with the copperhead is just trying to see it. Its neutral camouflage makes it inconspicuous in leaves and grass. The copperhead's color is hazel-brown above, with large crossbands of chestnut-brown. These bands are narrow on the snake's back and broad on its sides. The resulting pattern, when viewed from above, is like a series of hourglasses. Average length of a copperhead is about 30 inches.

On two occasions I have had copperheads come into camp. One got into a floorless tent, much to the surprise of its occupants. How long the snake had been in camp I can't say, but it was early morning when we found him lying next to a mattress.

It is said that the copperhead is the least deadly of the pit vipers found in this country, and I think that is probably true. I know several people who have been bitten by the copperhead. Though the experience was frightening and painful, the victims all lived to continue their outdoor interests.

Eastern Diamondback Rattlesnake—If you are going into swamps in the Deep South, the snake to watch out for is the eastern diamondback rattlesnake. Reaching lengths of 5 to 8 feet and weights up to 20 pounds, the eastern diamondback is North America's largest poisonous snake.

The range of the eastern diamondback is along the coastal areas of North and South Carolina; all of Florida; and the southern third of Georgia, Alabama, and Mississippi; and over to Louisiana. The snake's color is olive or grayish green or brown, with a chain of large diamond markings of a darker color surrounded

Largest poisonous snake in North America is the eastern diamondback rattler. It prefers the high ground in swamps but is a good swimmer. Credit: U.S. Fish & Wildlife Service.

by bright yellow borders about the width of a single scale.

During the 1960s, I had the opportunity to work closely with these snakes, and I learned to have a great deal of respect for them. They are usually found on high ground in and around swamps. During the cold months, the eastern diamondback will den up with other snakes, usually in the hole of a gopher tortoise. I have seen as many as 13 diamondbacks in one hole, averaging well over 5 feet in length. Though the diamondback likes the high ground in swamps, he is a good swimmer and will travel in the water.

The place to be especially watchful for these snakes is on islands and spots of dry land in the swamp, particularly during periods of high water. High water tends to crowd these creatures on any high, dry land. As with all snakes, be watchful where you walk and put your hands.

During the fall hunting season, these snakes are on the move. Don't make the mistake of watching for a squirrel in a tree and stepping on a diamondback. Most of the snakebite cases I've actually been involved with were the result of this snake. The victims were all hunters not watching where they were walking or (in the case of a wild-turkey hunter) sitting. I know of one swamp camper who was bitten by a large diamondback when he tried to kill it with a pop bottle. Treat the eastern diamondback with the caution you'd observe with any killer, because he is just that.

Canebrake Rattlesnake—One of the lesser-known snakes of the swamp is the canebrake rattlesnake, a cousin of the timber rattler. The canebrake rattler's range is the lower Mississippi Valley; from southeastern Texas;

The canebrake rattlesnake, which is more colorful than the eastern diamondback, is likely to be found in areas of darker, moist soils in which patches of cane grow. Credit: U.S. Fish & Wildlife Service.

north as far as Missouri and Illinois; and the lower elevations of the southeastern states, except the Florida peninsula, north to Virginia.

The canebrake's color is a gray or pinkish-gray body with black bands, with points directed backward like chevrons, and rusty red or yellow bands on the back. Unlike the diamondback rattler, the canebrake lives in areas of darker, moist soils, more particularly in patches of the cane that is the source of its name. This colorful rattlesnake grows to a length of over 8 feet.

For 3 years or more, I worked around canebrake rattlers almost every day. I noticed that they will give a man the right-of-way unless cornered. I also noticed that these snakes rattle very little. The swamp camper in the canebrake's range should use the same precautions as with the other poisonous snakes.

The species I've mentioned are the major poisonous snakes found in North American swamps, but it's possible that you'll run into others. Last year while trout fishing in a remote Virginia beaver miniswamp in the mountains, I started across the beaver dam and stopped when I saw three timber rattlers. There are swamps of one type or another in almost every poisonous snake's range. So during warm weather, a bit of caution is necessary. By thinking and watching, you can camp for a lifetime in swamps and never have a close call with a poisonous snake. Don't let snake tales keep you out of one of America's last great natural areas.

Snakebite Treatment—The proper treatment of a poisonous snakebite is still one of the most disputed subjects in the medical profession. The most accepted method of treatment, however, is the one advocated by Dr. Charles Watt of Thomasville, Georgia. Dr. Watt has been treating snakebite victims for 25 years and is recognized as one of the country's leading authorities on the subject. Here is Dr. Watt's recommended treatment.

1. Get away from the snake. It is not unusual for a snake to bite the victim several times.

2. Try to remain calm.

3. Positively identify the snake, and if possible get someone to kill the snake to take to the doctor so that it

can be identified and examined. That knowledge will be helpful in the treatment.

4. Make a constricting band out of a handkerchief, shirt sleeve, sock, belt, or even a rubberband. Put this band on above the bite (that is, between the bite and the body). It should be so loose that you can easily insert a finger under it. Such a constricting band will not stop the flow of blood through the artery, but it does check the return of blood through the veins and stops the fast spread of venom. Do not loosen this type of constricting band if you are within an hour of a doctor.

5. If you are within an hour's travel to a doctor, prepare the victim for the trip. Immobilize the bitten limb by putting on a splint. Make sure, however, that the splint's bindings are so loose that they do not impair circulation. If possible, keep the limb horizontal. The victim should not walk unless it is absolutely necessary; other members of the group should carry the victim to the vehicle or boat.

6. If you are more than an hour away from a doctor, a more complex procedure should be followed. Wash the wound with water, soap, alcohol, or whatever you have on hand. Make a short, straight incision (no cross cut) from one fang mark to the other and a little past each one. The cut should be no deeper than the fatty tissue under the skin. That's usually ⅛ of an inch. Use a sharp instrument that's been sterilized in the flame of a match.

7. If you have no cuts or sores in your mouth, suck the wound vigorously; or have someone else do it for you, if he can do so safely. Suction can remove 20 to 50 percent of the venom. A suction cup from a snakebit kit is useful if you are alone and the bite is an area you cannot reach with your mouth.

8. Apply a constricting band and a splint as directed

earlier (steps 4 and 5), and get medical treatment as quickly as possible. During the trip, it may be best to loosen the constricting band for 30 to 60 seconds every 15 minutes. Be cautious. People often go into shock when the constricting band is loosened, and this is especially true if the bite was made by a large snake.

Other points to remember concerning snakebite:

1. *Never* give a snakebite victim alcohol. It speeds up the flow of blood through the system and hastens the effect of the bite.

2. Immediately remove rings, bracelets, watches, shoes, or whatever from a bitten limb. The swelling will be fast, and such objects will constrict.

3. Absence of pain, swelling, or other symptoms does not necessarily mean that no venom has been injected. Bites that at first seem superficial can be fatal.

4. Most hospitals in snake country have antivenin for the treatment of snakebites. If a hospital doesn't have antivenin, they can call the Oklahoma Poison Information Center at (405) 271-5454. The center maintains a computerized inventory of antivenin available across the nation. *I keep this phone number taped in the lid of my first-aid kit.* Most likely I'll never need it, but it's there if I should.

5. Cottonmouths, rattlesnakes, and copperheads all belong to the family of snakes known as pit vipers. They have deep facial pits on each side of the head between the eye and nose. This sensory organ detects the approach of a warm-blooded animal and helps the pit viper to strike with deadly accuracy. Without this heat-seeking organ, these snakes would starve to death because they're somewhat slow moving and have poor eyesight. Contrary to popular belief, not all victims are struck by scared or angry snakes. Many sportsmen are hit by a hungry snake. The warm leg or arm was sensed

by the pits, and the snake struck, hoping it was a squirrel or rabbit.

6. Rattlesnakes don't always rattle before striking. In fact, some studies have shown that in 50 percent of the cases of rattlesnake bites, no rattle was heard.

7. Research is currently underway to find the perfect cure for snakebites. Researchers at Tulane Medical Center have found that the reason a venomous snake does not die from its own poison is that a clear protein substance in the snake's blood makes him immune. The scientists have isolated the substance and are trying to develop a new antitoxin for humans.

Also a Texas A & I researcher has discovered that the southwestern wood rat's blood chemistry enables it to share a burrow with diamondback rattlesnakes and withstand the shock of their venomous bites. Mice, which are much less immune to the venom, were injected with cells from wood-rat blood. The blood serum increased protection in the mice by a factor of 3.6. Scientists hope to isolate and purify the protective factor to see if this apparent transfer property will apply to other animals and humans.

Maybe by the time this book is revised I will be able to tell you how to treat snakebite with a foolproof cure.

BUGS AND HOW TO COPE WITH THEM

Nothing can spoil a swamp trip quicker than an attack from flying or crawling pests. If you're properly prepared, you can live with these pests under most circumstances and have little discomfort. But if you go unprepared into the swamp, you can literally be putting your life on the line.

Mosquitoes—Recently I was asked to lead a search for two canoeists who were overdue from a 1-day trip into south Alabama river swamp. The pair hadn't taken along any survival gear, and they had chosen a swamp that was impossible to cross in 1 day during a period of low water. We found the overdue canoeists early the next morning. They had spent the night without the aid of fire, shelter, or insect repellent. They were swollen so badly from the hundreds of mosquito bites that we had to rush them to a nearby hospital.

Every swamp camper should know that during the warm months any swamp is going to have mosquitoes. Plan accordingly. Not only are these flying pests a nuisance; their bites can be dangerous.

There are over 1,600 kinds of mosquitoes in the world, at least 120 of which live here in North America. The female mosquito needs a high-protein meal in a liquid form before she is able to lay her eggs. The handiest liquid high-protein meal available is blood. In order to find a meal, the mosquito has sensors that are attracted to warm, moist objects. The skin temperature and moisture of one person can differ markedly from the skin temperature and moisture of another. Consequently, mosquitoes are attracted to some people more than to others.

Sight also plays a big part in the mosquito's location of prey. A mosquito sees best whatever objects contrast most strongly with the background. Shiny fabrics and pale colors are easier for them to see than dull-surfaced dark clothing. Sportsmen wearing camouflage clothing have noticed that they are not bothered as much by mosquitoes as when they wear light-blue denim. It is also of interest to note that researchers have found that people in motion get bitten more often than those who are standing still.

The best way to live in the mosquitoes' environment is to go prepared to keep them away from you. There are several good repellents available that will keep these flying pests at a comfortable distance. The one I prefer is Deep Woods Off, a Johnson Wax Product. This repellent seems to last longer than others and comes in handy towelettes, which can be easily carried by sportsmen. Another good repellent is put out by Cutter.

Louisiana outdoor writer Frank Davis tells me that a trapper in his state, who makes his living walking the marshes, has discovered a new way to keep mosquitoes away. He uses "Skin-So-Soft" by Avon. It's inexpensive, keeps you from getting wind burn, and doesn't take the finish off your gun. Most of all, he claims, the mosquitoes hate it.

It should be noted here that you should keep commercial repellents away from fly lines, rod finishes, and mono line because the repellent will dissolve them. I lost a nice bass recently because my 20-pound-test mono line snapped where a drop of insect repellent had fallen onto the line spool. Repellents will take the finish off gun stocks. And I'm told that if you get insect repellent on fishing flies and lures, fish can detect the odor and be repelled.

Another method of keeping mosquitoes (and your friends) at bay is to eat a big dose of garlic. The odor is secreted through the skin and repels insects.

If you are likely to be bitten by mosquitoes, you should have a bottle of calamine lotion in your first-aid kit. This lotion has a soothing effect.

Under no circumstances should the swamp camper go into a swamp without protection from mosquitoes. You should have a good supply of repellent, wear a long-sleeved shirt and long pants of a dark color, and always carry a supply of waterproof matches. Had the two canoeists who got lost in the Alabama swamp had matches, they could have built a smoky fire for some relief.

My guide and I once had to spend the night, unexpectedly, in a mosquito-infested Michigan swamp. The guide built two smoky fires, and we slept between them. We were bitten, but not nearly as badly as we would have been without the fires.

Ticks—Ticks are found around most of our swamps, and all campers should be especially watchful for them during the warm months. The two most common ticks are the Lonestar tick and the American Dog tick. These ticks can transmit germs of several diseases, including Rocky Mountain Spotted Fever, a disease that occurs in the eastern United States as well as the west.

Everyone should be able to recognize the symptoms of Rocky Mountain Spotted Fever, which may appear from 2 to 12 days after the bite by an infected tick. Early signs of the disease are sudden chills, high fever, severe headache, and other aches and pains. A distinct spotted rash, which may be mistaken for measles, usually appears on approximately the third day of the disease. The rash begins on the wrists, ankles, and back.

This tick-borne illness can be very effectively treated with antibiotics if it's detected early. Treatment is neither painful nor complicated.

A person may be bitten by a tick without knowing it and later infected with Rocky Mountain Spotted Fever. So at the first sign of these symptoms, a physician should be called. Make sure he knows the patient was exposed to a tick-infested area. Not all ticks are carriers of Rocky Mountain Spotted Fever. Even in heavily infested areas, in fact, only about 1 tick in 20 is able to transmit the disease.

I can't remember a year when I didn't find a dozen or

more ticks on me during the summer, and I've never suffered any ill effects. But on the first camping trip my wife went on with me, she picked up a tick in her hair that we didn't find for several days. Sure enough, she came down with the fever. It didn't discourage her from camping, but now she keeps a sharp eye out for ticks.

The first line of defense against ticks is to use a commercial insect repellent that specifies effectiveness against ticks. I know of one swamp guide who wears cat tick-flea collars around his wrists and ankles for tick protection. He swears it works.

Since ticks are found in grass and on bushes, the camper should make it a common practice to check himself thoroughly for ticks at least once each day. A methodical check should be made on the hairy parts of the body, especially the head.

If a tick is found attached to the body, you should cover the tick with heavy oil, such as mineral or salad oil, to close its breathing pores. The tick may release its hold at once; if not, allow the oil to stay on the tick for 30 minutes. Then remove the tick with tweezers from your first-aid kit, making sure all parts are removed. Wash the bite area with soap and water.

Stinging Insects—A sting from the hymenoptera order of insects—bees, yellow jackets, hornets, wasps—can be dangerous. Some 50 deaths a year from these stings are recorded in the United States, and many doctors believe the real figure is far higher. Surprising to many sportsmen, there are far more fatalities from stings than from snakebite.

Among the greatest dangers in swamps are the large nests of paper wasps, which reach the size of a man's hat and are built in bushes that hang over the water. The careless fisherman can get into trouble fast if he accidentally disturbs one. If you're keeping your eyes open for cottonmouths, you'll spot these nests.

Also be especially careful in selecting a campsite. Scout the area carefully, and be observant for yellow-jacket nests. Yellow jackets build their nests in the ground and are particularly fond of old stumps. Many times the nest opening is one small hole, and it is difficult to see. I once started putting up my backpack tent over a yellow-jacket nest. I had to sneak back after dark to get the tent.

Insects of the hymenoptera order inject venom under the skin when they sting. Under normal conditions the venom produces a few minutes of burning followed by itching and reddening at the sting site. Ice or calamine lotion will normally remedy the situation.

To the person who is venom-sensitive, however, the situation is extremely serious. Such a person may experience labored breathing, swallowing difficulty, chest constriction, abdominal pain, nausea, weakness, and unconsciousness. This person (it is estimated that 8 out of every 1,000 people are venom-sensitive) is in trouble and needs help fast. Any sportsman who knows he is venom-sensitive should get his doctor to prescribe a sting-kit. In the swamp, it could save his life.

The best prevention is to follow these simple rules.

1. Watch for nests of bees, wasps, hornets, and yellow jackets. If you find such a nest, leave the area quickly and quietly.

2. Wear shoes and socks when walking around the campsite.

3. Avoid the use of scented soaps, lotions, perfumes, and the like. These attract stinging insects.

4. Avoid bright-colored clothes.

5. Keep a clean camp and do not leave food stuffs open. Keep your garbage tightly sealed.
6. Don't swat at stinging insects.
7. Use insect repellent.

Chiggers—Chiggers (or red bugs, as they are commonly called) are a common pest around summer campsites. These tiny red pests burrow into the skin to feed, and they create an intense itching. Usually their bites are only a small discomfort. But things were different on a bowhunt for deer on Blackbeard Island off the coast of Georgia, when a hunting companion of mine took a nap in the woods. The next day he was covered with chigger bites, and medical attention was a must.

Chiggers can be avoided by treating your clothing with sulphur dust. Something else that works well is to apply commercial insect repellent to clothing and exposed skin. Once a chigger bite is discovered, an application of clear fingernail polish will usually bring about a quick remedy.

Spiders—There are two spiders of which swamp campers should beware: (1) the black widow, and (2) the brown recluse.

The black widow is found in damp, dark places where insects are abundant. I have seen them in hollow trees, under boat seats, under rocks, and in campgrounds under the seat of a pit toilet. Only the female is poisonous. She is dark black with red markings in the form of an hourglass on the underside of the abdomen. Man is seldom bitten by this spider, but if you're bitten, it is serious. The bite symptoms are severe pain, profuse

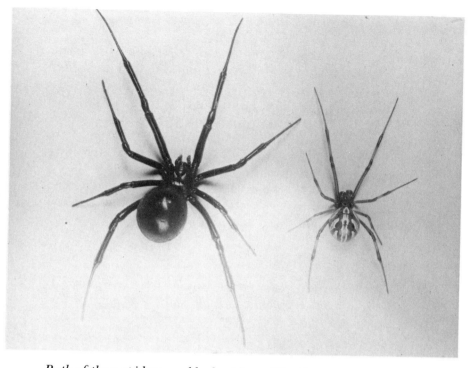

Both of these spiders are black widows. The big one at the left is a female; the other is a male. Only the female is poisonous. She has an identifying red hourglass-shaped mark on the underside of the abdomen. Credit: U.S.D.A.

sweating, nausea, painful cramps of abdominal muscles, and difficult breathing.

Treatment of the bite should be left to a doctor. In transporting the victim, keep him warm and as calm as possible. Apply cold compresses to the bite area.

The brown recluse spider (also called the brown spider or fiddleback spider) varies in color from gray-brown to deep red-brown. The most noticeable mark is a dark, fiddle-shaped area on the front half of its back. Its leg span is about the size of a half dollar. This spider likes dry, dark areas and is especially fond of shoes, clothing, sleeping bags, and rolled-up tents.

Incidentally, it is always a good policy to shake out camp clothing and shoes before you put them on. One of the largest black widows I've ever seen came rolling out of my waders one morning.

Symptoms of the brown recluse bite include intense local pain, a blister at the bite site, inflammation of the affected area, and an ulcerating sore.

The brown recluse spider varies in color from gray-brown to deep red-brown. Its most noticeable mark is a dark, fiddle-shaped area on the front half of its back. Credit: U.S.D.A.

Treatment should be the same as for the black-widow bite: get the victim to a doctor, keeping him warm and as calm as possible. Apply cold compresses to the bite area.

Most of the spiders you will encounter in the swamp are harmless. In fact, many swamp campers spend a lifetime visiting swamps and never see a poisonous spider.

LIGHTNING—KILLER FROM ABOVE

A summer thunderstorm in a swamp can be one of the most frightening experiences in a sportman's lifetime, and with good reason. Lightning is a well-known killer.

Several years ago, I was guiding an Ohio fisherman in a swamp in east Texas when a sudden and fierce thunderstorm hit. Since we were caught out in some tall timber, I asked my client to lie down in the boat as I was going to crank the motor and move into a strand of thick, low-growing brush. He was shocked that I would even think of putting the boat into that "cottonmouth-infested brush."

As he was preaching to me the dangers of snakes, a bolt of lightning clobbered a nearby cypress with an ear-splitting crack. Pieces of bark flew in all directions. My client dived to the bottom of the boat and begged me to get into the low-growing bushes. The storm lasted 2 long hours with the severity of a mortar attack. On the way back to camp my pale client told me that snakes were now only his second swamp fear—lightning was first!

Lightning kills more people in the United States than either snakebites, tornadoes, floods, or hurricanes.

Each year an average of 200 people are killed by lightning. Many of these are outdoorsmen in swamps.

A recent study dealing with the analysis of deaths and injuries from lightning during the 20-year period 1950 through 1969 found that of the 2,054 people killed by lightning and the 4,156 injured, 24 percent of those killed and 23 percent of those injured were outdoor recreationists. Of those 494 recreationists who were killed, 36 were campers or picnickers, 39 were shore or bank fishermen, 33 were fishing in boats, and 30 were pleasure boating.

It should be of interest to those of us who hunt, fish, and camp in southern swamps that there is a higher-than-average incidence of lightning fatalities and injuries along the Mississippi River and the Gulf Coast. The area around Tampa, Florida, is especially lightning prone. However, this is not to say that any area cannot produce deadly lightning under the right conditions.

How can you avoid death or injury from lightning?

First, of course, is to get the latest weather forecast before embarking on a recreational outing. If there is a chance of thunderstorms, take a small battery-operated radio along to get occasional updates. Be ready to seek shelter if a severe thunderstorm watch or warning is announced. The more severe the thunderstorm, the greater the intensity and frequency of lightning strokes.

By all means develop the habit of keeping a weather eye on the sky. You don't need an official warning to tell you a thunderstorm is coming. In almost all cases, you can see the towering thunderhead and occasional flashes of lightning at least a half hour in advance. Usually this is ample time to find shelter or take precautions.

When a thunderstorm threatens, all lightning experts agree that the most important single thing you can do is to get inside a house or a large building or inside an all-metal vehicle. Outdoor recreationists frequently overlook the fact that their all-metal automobile or pickup truck is an excellent lightning shelter. Even if it's struck, the vehicle allows the current to be discharged harmlessly into the ground.

But what about the times you're deep in a swamp and don't have time to reach a safe building or an automobile. According to the National Weather Bureau, under these circumstances:

• Do not stand underneath a natural lightning rod such as a large tree in an open area.

• Avoid projecting above the surrounding landscape, as you would do if you were standing on a hilltop, in an open field, or fishing from a small boat.

• Get out of and away from open water. (If you're swimming, the current from a nearby lightning stroke can flow through the water to you.)

• Stay away from wire fences, clothes lines, metal pipes, rails, and other metallic paths which could carry lightning to you from some distance away.

• Avoid standing in small isolated sheds or other small structures in open areas.

• In a swamp, seek shelter in a low area under a thick growth of small trees. In open areas, go to a low place such as a ravine or valley.

• If you're hopelessly isolated in an open area and you feel your hair stand on end—indicating lightning is about to strike—drop to your knees and bend forward, putting your hands on your knees. Then if lightning strikes near you, the chances of its using your body as a conductor are minimized.

• Groups of persons (such as campers) in exposed

situations should spread out so that if lightning strikes nearby, the smallest number will be affected.

Many people apparently "killed" by lightning can be revived if quick action is taken. When a group is affected, the apparently dead should be treated first. Those unconscious but breathing will probably recover spontaneously.

According to the American Red Cross, first-aid should be given to those not breathing within 4 to 6 minutes or less, to prevent irrevocable damage to the brain. Mouth-to-mouth resuscitation should be administered once very 5 seconds to adults and once every 3 seconds to infants and small children, until medical help arrives.

If the victim is not breathing and has no pulse, cardiopulmonary resuscitation is necessary. This is a combination of mouth-to-mouth resuscitation and external cardiac compression. It should be administered by persons with proper training. The technique can be learned from local Red Cross or Heart Association chapters in 1-day sessions.

Medical attention also should be given to victims who seem only temporarily stunned or otherwise unhurt, since there may be hidden effects.

In a swamp situation, the best precaution is to keep an eye on the weather at all times and have a selected place to go if a thunderstorm strikes. Don't tie your boat to a tall cypress tree. Take shelter in a clump of low-growing bushes. Also be cautious of where you set up camp. Don't camp under tall trees that serve as lightning rods.

SUMMERTIME KILLER—HEAT

One of the most commonly overlooked dangers in the summer swamp is, simply, heat. The temperature is high, the humidity is high, and there is little or no breeze. Chances are you're not accustomed to such heat or to the hard work of pulling a loaded canoe over logs, winching a jeep out of mud, or paddling a boat through shallow water. These conditions can bring on the deadly condition known as heat stroke or the less serious condition known as heat exhaustion. A person does not have to be in the sun to get either of these conditions. A hot, shaded swamp can be enough.

Heat Stroke—energy production in the human body is accompanied by the production of excess heat. To eliminate this heat, the body increases the flow of blood through the skin and stimulates the production of sweat—the body's air conditioner. Through evaporation, convection, and radiation, the body gets rid of excess heat. If a malfunction occurs in the heat-regulating mechanism, the body temperature can zoom to 110°F. Then the body's vital organs—brain, heart, and kidneys—literally cook in their own juices. The result is death. Every year in this country an average of 4,000 deaths are attributed to heat stroke.

Heat stroke can come on with little warning. However, the symptoms are usually headache, dizziness, lack of sweating, *dry, hot,* and *red skin,* fast strong pulse, constricted pupils, and high temperature.

Treatment for heat strokes is as follows:

1. Move the victim to a cool place and lay him down with his head raised.

2. Open the clothes and cool the body down quickly, using every means possible.

3. Get the victim to a doctor as soon as possible.

Heat Exhaustion—Heat exhaustion, while less serious than heat stroke, is nothing to ignore. If not treated, heat exhaustion will most likely develop into heat stroke.

The symptoms of heat exhaustion are weakness, muscle cramps, headaches, profuse sweating, *pale, cool, clammy skin*—as opposed to hot and dry, and red skin with heat stroke—and normal temperature.

Treament for heat exhaustion is as follows:

1. Move the victim to a cool place and lay him down with the feet slightly raised.

2. Give him slightly salted water to drink.

3. If recovery is not quick, get him to a doctor.

Prevention of Heat Danger—The best way to cope with the dangers of heat stroke and heat exhaustion is to prevent them. Here are the rules you should follow to prevent heat disorders.

1. Before you go on a swamp-camping trip during the summer, spend 2 weeks getting acclimated to high temperatures and heavy exertion. For an hour each day, exercise in the heat. Start out slowly, and rest often. Remember, heavy exertion in hot climates uses up a lot of the body's liquids. Drink large quantities of Gatorade and bouillon.

2. Avoid drugs that promote heat stroke or reduce your natural thirst. Check with your doctor if you are

taking sedatives, diuretics, tranquilizers, and such. Go easy on all forms of alcoholic drinks. If you're running a fever, stay home.

3. Wear lightweight, loose-fitting clothing that is white or light tan. Be sure to wear a hat, but make sure that it is ventilated to promote evaporative cooling from the sweat-soaked hair. Be careful when wearing rain gear. It tends to trap body heat.

4. Stop frequently to cool off. Try wetting your hair.

5. Save heavy chores for early morning and late afternoon, when the air is cooler. Relax during the heat of the day.

6. Make sure your liquid intake replaces your sweat output. The body requires 2 quarts of water per day: 1 quart to moisten lung air, 1 pint for urine, and 1 pint for perspiration. Dehydration is an important factor in causing heat disorders.

7. Many doctors now tell us to avoid salt pills. Eat foods such as nuts, chocolate bars with nuts, tomato juice, V-8 juice, bouillon, and dried raisins. The body usually requires 1 to 3 grams of salt daily to replace the salt lost in urine. This lost salt must be replaced, since the body does not make any.

QUICKSAND—A SWAMP MYTH

One reason that many sportsmen give for avoiding the excellent hunting and fishing available in swamps is that they're worried about getting into quicksand. The pulsating beds of quicksand we have all seen on the silver screen at the local theater have misled many would-be swamp visitors into thinking they'll be swallowed up if they make the wrong step.

During all of my years of swamp travel and camping

I have never seen a bed of quicksand. In order to check the subject further, I recently spent some time with Charles Laney of Tuscaloosa, Alabama, a soils engineer, who has spent years studying swamp soils and hunting and fishing in swamps throughout North America. Charles tells me that quicksand is more myth than fact, particularly in swamps. Furthermore, he states that quicksand is a condition and not a soil type.

Gravels, sands, and silts become "quick" when an upward flow of ground water takes place to such an extent that the particles are lifted.

When the uplift pressure and total stress are in balance, the mass may look deceptively stable. However, a machine or structure on the soil surface will sink slowly if it's heavier than the saturated soil. This condition would normally occur in areas around a spring that has been silted-in. But it would be in only the immediate area of the artesian flow and would present no danger to humans. Quicksand as depicted in T.V. dramas and movies is generally accepted by soil scientists as purely an overdramatization of an unlikely situation in North American swamps.

I don't mean to imply that there aren't some bogs and mud deposits in which you'll sink. I have seen bogs in the Rockies above timberline in which you could sink a horse up to his belly. I have also seen mud, especially in overused wet logging roads, where you could sink up to your knees. The same holds true in silt-laden stream bottoms. When proper precaution is used, however, none of these situations presents a problem to a swamp traveler.

If you have been avoiding swamps for fear of quicksand, cheer up. Quicksand is seen only on your T.V. set, not in the swamp.

HYPOTHERMIA

Most sportsmen think that the deadliest killer in swamps is quicksand or poisonous snakes. That view is far from correct. Each year more sportsmen get into trouble or die in swamps because of the condition that nowadays is called hypothermia. Hypothermia is the lowering of the body's core temperature. We are all familiar with the fact that our normal core temperature is 98.6°F. But what many sportsmen don't know is that any lowering of this core temperature is dangerous.

It doesn't require freezing weather for a sportsman to get hypothermia. The danger can occur on a 50°F day in Florida just as easily as it can at freezing temperatures in Maine. During the 20 years I have worked in swamps, I have seen only five sportsmen bitten by poisonous snakes and have never known anyone to get into quicksand. But I have seen and helped bring out scores of hypothermia victims. Hypothermia is a sneaky killer.

Here's a typical example of how hypothermia can slowly kill you without your knowing it. You're on a fall bowhunt for deer in a swamp in western Kentucky. The air temperature is not very cold. It's been between 30 and 50°F. all day, so you're dressed in a cotton camouflage suit. You're tired, the wind has started blowing, and a drizzle of rain has started to fall.

You start the long walk back to the camp, and soon you start feeling the cold. First you begin to shiver, and then the shivering becomes uncontrollable. You feel weak and nauseated, so you stop to sit down. Your hunting buddy wants to know why you've stopped. You have trouble speaking clearly, and your movements and thinking have become sluggish.

You and your buddy haven't recognized it, but you've got hypothermia. Already your body temperature has dropped to 94°F. While your buddy kids you about not being man enough to take it and looks for material to build a fire, your temperature continues to fall.

Your body temperature is at 90°F. The shivering decreases, and thinking becomes fuzzier. Your temperature falls to 85°F., and you become irrational.

Your buddy, not knowing what's wrong, starts trying to lead you to camp. Your temperature continues to drop. When it hits 80°F, you're unconscious. Your buddy leaves to find help. Soon after he leaves, your temperature drops to 77°F. and you die.

What killed you directly was the cold. But the indirect cause of death was your failure to think about what you were getting into before you went on that hunt. You were not prepared.

This same lack of forethought and preparation kills hunters, canoeists, fishermen, and others in the outdoors each year. Hypothermia can strike in any season and any climate. All that is needed is a mild air temperature (30 to 50°F.) wetness (be it rain, sweat, or a river dunking), a slight wind, and a tired person.

Hypothermia attacks a person in two steps. The first is when your body begins to lose heat faster than it produces heat. At this point you're aware of feeling cold, and the shivering begins.

The second step is when the cold reaches your brain, depriving you of judgment and reasoning power. This is why almost nobody recognizes that he has hypothermia. In this second step, your internal temperature is sliding downward. Without treatment, this slide leads to stupor, collapse, and death.

The onset of hypothermia is usually slow. But in boating accidents it can happen quickly. In 1968, nine of the toughest, strongest, and best-trained canoeists in the world were paddling across the Potomac River at Quantico, Virginia, when their canoe capsized. Fifteen minutes later, all of them were dead—victims of hypothermia.

This Marine canoe team died so fast because they had been paddling their 25-foot canoe at a racing pace for more than 4 miles before they capsized. Their blood circulation was rapid, they were tired, and their cotton sweatsuits were soaked. The day itself was warm and sunny for March. But when the canoeists hit the 40°F. water, their body heat drained away so fast that they probably were helpless within 2 or 3 minutes. When your body is immersed in cold water, you'll start losing heat fast. In 2 minutes your skin temperature will drop to within 3°F. of the water temperature.

Since much of swamp travel is over water, the swamp camper must understand the dangers of hypothermia from falling into cold water. According to the U.S. Coast Guard—based on research by Dr. Martin Collis, University of Victoria, British Columbia—survival in cold water depends on many factors. The temperature of the water is only one factor. Others include body size, fat, and activity in the water. Large people cool slower than small people. Fat people cool slower than thin people. Children, because they are small, cool faster than adults. Anyone swimming or treading water cools faster than those who remain still.

In case of accidental immersion in cold water, remember that water conducts heat much faster than air. Most boats will float, even when capsized or swamped. So get in or on the boat to get as far out of the water as possible. Wearing a life jacket is a *must*. A proper one will keep you afloat even if you're unconscious. Remaining still and assuming a fetal posture (Heat Escape Lessening Posture—HELP) will increase survival time. About 50 percent of the heat is lost from the head, according to the U.S. Coast Guard. It is therefore important to keep the head out of the water.

Stay with the boat. Even a capsized boat is easier for rescuers to spot than a person in the water. If several people are in the water, huddling close side-to-side in a circle will help preserve body heat.

This position is what's called the HELP (heat escape lessening posture).

There are several ways to avoid an accident that can cause hypothermia. When traveling by boat or canoe, avoid standing or moving around. Do not overload or improperly distribute your boat's load. Avoid sudden high-speed turns. Watch for obstacles in the water.

When you are traveling over land or in camp, follow these precautions against hypothermia:

1. Stay dry. When clothes get wet, they lose about 90 percent of their insulating value. Wool loses less than 90 percent of its insulating value; cotton, down, and synthetics lose more. Avoid sweating, carry rain gear, and avoid falling into water.

2. Beware of the wind. A slight breeze carries heat away from bare skin much faster than does still air. Wind drives cold air under and through clothing. Wind refrigerates wet clothes by evaporating moisture from the surface.

3. Understand cold. Most hypothermia cases develop in air temperatures between 30 and 50°F. Most outdoorsmen simply can't believe such temperatures can be dangerous. They may fatally underestimate the danger of being wet at such temperatures.

4. End your exposure. When you cannot stay dry and warm under existing weather conditions, be smart enough to call it quits and return to camp or home.

5. Never ignore shivering. Persistent or violent shivering is clear warning that you are on the verge of hypothermia.

The symptoms of hypothermia are obvious. Watch for them in yourself and in others.

• Uncontrollable fits of shivering.
• Vague, slow, slurred speech.

- Lapses in memory.
- Immobile, fumbling hands.
- Staggering and stumbling.
- Drowsiness.
- Exhaustion, inability to get up after a rest.

In most cases, the victim will deny he's in trouble. But believe the symptoms, not the victim. Treatment should be immediate.

1. Get the victim into a sheltered area.
2. Remove all wet clothing.
3. If the victim is only mildly impaired:
   a. give him warm drinks, and
   b. get him into dry clothes and a warm car, room, or sleeping bag.
4. If the victim is semiconscious or worse and does not have the capability of regaining his body temperature without outside help:
   a. keep him awake and give warm drinks;
   b. leave him stripped and put him in a sleeping bag with another person also stripped—skin-to-skin contact is the most effective treatment; and
   c. if the victim seems dead, heart massage (CPR) and mouth-to-mouth resuscitation should be administered.

Hypothermia has been called the killer of the unprepared. So on your next swamp-camping trip and on every trip, think hypothermia and go prepared!

ALLIGATORS, BEARS, AND BLACK PANTHERS

Movies and television have done a lot to scare people into thinking all swamps are full of creatures waiting for a tasty human meal. Next to quicksand and snakes, the category I call alligators, bears, and black panthers is the reason given by most sportsmen to stay out of game-and-fish-rich swamps. Let's take a look at these misjudged critters.

Alligators—First of all, alligators are found only in the Deep South. The American alligator has had his range so reduced by poachers and developers that he is rarely seen except on protected government land. Where alligators are found, they're interesting to watch. The only time I have seen alligators appear to be dangerous is when they are threatened, when someone gets too close to a nest or to the little alligators, or when people try to get too close to semiwild alligators to feed them.

The only time I have seen an alligator to be a threat to sportsmen was several years ago in the Okefenokee Swamp. Ed Stell, a swamp-camping friend who is a native of Michigan, and I were fishing for large bowfin on the west side of the swamp. We were using heavy tackle: 20-pound-test line and large spinners. We noticed several large 'gators sunning in the water within casting distance of our boat. When I made a long cast near a particularly large 'gator, the wind blew my line over his nose. I took up line, easing the spinner up to the 'gator's nose, and gave a slight jerk to flip the spinner over his snout. Rather than flip, the spinner stuck in his nose. Instantly the 'gator started splashing

If you're lucky enough to spot an alligator, you'll find it interesting to watch. But don't crowd it or give it the impression that you might be threatening it.

and twisting. I had my hands full because the 'gator was coming toward the rocking boat. As I reached for my knife to cut the line, the spinner came loose. The hook had straightened. The 'gator blew at us and swam off in complete disgust, much to our relief!

Other than that one instance, which was my fault, I have spent weeks around alligators where we all lived in harmony. When I'm in 'gator country, I don't hang fish over the side of the boat. I also make sure the 'gators hear my coming so that I don't surprise them.

Bears—Black bears and swamps go together like mud and children. In many areas of North America, swamps are the last holdouts for black bears. I have never known anyone camping in a swamp to have a dangerous encounter with a black bear. I have had my camp torn down by a bear, and I know of others who have suffered the same fate. If we had kept our food and garbage stored out of reach, the bears would not have come into camp. Other than finding an easy meal, black bears ordinarily don't want anything to do with people.

If a bear comes into camp, snap on a light, bang on a pan, or do something else to let him know you're there. Be cautious not to get between a mother and her cub. Unless it's cornered, or its cubs seem to be threatened, a bear will leave when it finds out you're there.

Black Panthers—Almost every swamp has its black-panther tale. Since there are no black panthers in North America what can I say except don't believe stories about black panthers? Most swamps are blessed with bobcats, but they don't want anything to do with a camper. In the South, the Florida panther (the eastern mountain lion) seems to be making a slow comeback in some swamps. But you will probably never see one. Like bobcats, these big cats stay away from people.

In short, the alligator, bear, and black panther category of "swamp killers" grows more from campfire talk than from reality. I would hate to know some well-deserving sportsman missed a swamp outing because of these fears.

DEEP WATER

Swamps, like lakes, are water environments. Contrary to the belief of many people, you can drown just as easily in a swamp as you can in any other body of water. River swamps run swift during periods of heavy rain. Most swamps have deep holes, and boating accidents occur in swamps just about as they do on lakes. Many swamp campers think that swamps are only 2 or 3 feet deep. Many times this belief is accurate, but there may be another 2 or 3 feet of soft silt and mud on the bottom, making wading out impossible.

Swamp campers, like boaters everywhere, should know how to swim. You should always have a life jacket (personal flotation device) when you're in a boat or canoe. You should also use the same precautions when boating or canoeing that you'd use in any other body of water.

Last, but far from least, you should know how to administer artificial respiration. Just because swamps seem shallow, don't let them fool you into using poor judgment. A swamp should be treated with the same precautions and respect as a deep lake.

HEART ATTACK

As more and more people discover the adventure and excitement of swamp hunting and fishing, the more we hear of heart attacks in swamps. Unlike camping in a recreational vehicle, swamp camping and other swamp activities are more involved and require us to be in better physical condition.

The weekend outdoorsman who spends most of his time behind a desk and suddenly decides to go into the cedar swamps of Michigan for a hard week of deer hunting is asking for trouble. Swamp camping involves paddling a canoe over and around obstacles for miles, getting a four-wheel-drive vehicle unstuck time after time, cutting wood, walking for miles, wading over rough terrain, and on and on. How many occasional swamp campers over 35 are in shape for these activities?

Each year I have the grim task of looking for overdue hunters and fishermen in the swamps where I work. Many who are overdue are the victims of heart attacks. If you ever have to bring the body of a fellow duck hunter miles out of a swamp to a waiting ambulance and family, you will know just how serious a heart attack is.

Each year more than one million Americans are felled by heart attacks. Of this number more than 670,000 die. Many hundreds of these victims are outdoorsmen—people a lot like you and me who just aren't in shape or prepared for the rigors of exploring swamps.

According to the American Heart Association, the first step toward avoiding a heart attack is to adjust your living habits so as to have a healthy heart. They suggest these six things to remember.

1. Reduce saturated fat and cholesterol in your diet. Have frequent meals of fish and poultry, which contain less saturated fat than meat. If you've been looking for an excuse to get into a swamp and do more fishing and wild-turkey hunting, now you have it. When serving

meat, use lean cuts and trim off fat. Also eat fewer eggs. Use skim milk, and cook with liquid vegetable oils.

2. Count your calories—avoid excess weight. If you tend to be overweight, ask your doctor for a sensible reducing diet.

3. Control high blood pressure. Have your blood pressure checked regularly.

4. Don't smoke. The heart-attack death rate among men is 50 percent to 200 percent higher for cigarette smokers than for nonsmokers.

5. Exercise regularly. Your doctor can tell you what kind of exercise will suit your age and physical condition.

6. Have regular medical checkups.

The swamp traveler, especially if he is an office worker, over 35 years old, or both should begin preparing for the forthcoming trip several months in advance. His first step of preparation will be a complete medical checkup, including an "exercise electrocardiogram." This test is given while you are under stress on a stationary bicycle or treadmill while a cardiologist monitors your heart and blood pressure continuously. The results tell you just how much strenuous exercise you can safely take.

While you are at your doctor's, tell him of your swamp hunting and fishing plans. Ask him to recommend exercise to strengthen your heart, legs, lungs, and such so that your trip will be safe and enjoyable.

Your doctor will probably prescribe your exercise with the same precision as any other medical treatment, with specific periods, frequencies, and intensities spelled out. Based on your current health, age, and exercise-electrocardiogram results, you will be placed on a program of walking, jogging, swimming, bicycling, or rope skipping that will condition your cardiovascular system for the type of swamp activity in which you will be participating. Your doctor probably will also encourage you to use steps rather than elevators, an excellent exercise for outdoorsmen. An outstanding booklet entitled "Exercise Your Way To Fitness And Heart Health" is available through your local heart association.

After your checkup, start your exercise program immediately and stay with it. The outdoorsman who waits to begin training until the week before he shoves off into some remote swamp is asking for trouble.

The second step toward preparing for swamp activities should be to take a Red Cross first-aid training course or Heart Association course that includes treatment for heart attacks. A course of this type will qualify you to carry out cardiopulmonary resuscitation, commonly known as CPR. CPR is the combination of artificial respiration and manual artificial circulation that is recommended for use if somebody's heart stops (cardiac arrest). CPR requires special training in the recognition of cardiac arrest and in the performing of the proper treatment. Instruction includes practice on a mannequin in performing both individually and as part of a team. Encourage your outdoor buddies to take the course with you because the *first* heart attack turns out to be fatal for almost 40 percent of the victims, and 20 percent of the victims of first heart attacks die in the first hour. Knowing what to do in a swamp could save the life of you or your friend.

The following treatment is recommended by the American National Red Cross for heart attacks.

1. If the victim is unconscious and not breathing, begin artificial respiration or (if a qualified person is there) CPR at once.

2. If the victim is conscious, place him in a comfortable position—usually sitting up—particularly if there is a shortness of breath. His comfort is a good guide.

3. Provide ventilation and guard against drafts and cold.

4. Have someone go for help: call for an ambulance equipped with oxygen, and have the victim's personal doctor notified.

5. If the victim has been under medical care, help him with his prescribed medicine. If the victim is unconscious, look for some form of emergency identification. If you're in doubt, confer with a doctor by telephone as soon as possible.

6. Do not give liquids to an unconscious victim. If he is conscious, do not give him cold liquid. It passes down the esophagus and chills the back part of the heart. This chilling can cause the blood vessels supplying the heart muscle to contract, thereby reducing the amount of blood flow to the heart, which is already in trouble.

7. Since transportation throws added strain upon the victim, do not attempt to transport him until you get medical advice. Today there are well-trained and well-equipped rescue teams in almost every county in the United States. Call them immediately, and try to keep calm. Do not let panic cause you to take unnecessary chances by trying to carry the victim out unaided.

If you have had a heart problem or go into swamps with someone who has, keep these simple rules in mind:
• Never go into a swamp alone.
• Avoid alcohol.
• Avoid heavy camp duties.

• Take a nap after lunch.
• Avoid activities in hot, humid weather.
• Move at a slow pace.
• Avoid unnecessary exertion such as pulling a loaded canoe over a log or dragging out a deer.
• Always let your fellow hunters, guide, and outfitter know about your problem.

Swamp activities are not supposed to be an endurance test, so slow down and enjoy it by following these rules and your doctor's advice. You can enjoy swamp camping even with a history of a heart problem.

Every day, on the average, heart disease kills 1,400 Americans. Strokes take another 500 lives. In total, the toll is more than a life a minute, and hundreds of thousands are crippled every year. Strenuous swamp activities can put an out-of-condition outdoorsmen in these numbers. Start this year to condition your body to combat the killer of outdoorsmen—heart attack!

POISON PLANTS

If you spend much time in swamps, sooner or later you'll come into contact with a member of the Rhus family. Rhus is the scientific name of North American plants that includes poison sumac, common poison ivy, and oakleaf poison ivy. Western poison oak is also a member of this family, but since it is not usually found in swamps it is omitted here.

Many swamp campers spend years around these plants and suffer no ill effects. Then suddenly they begin to itch. No one seems to be always immune to the Rhus plants. One reason the old "swamp rats" seem to be immune is that they recognize the various plants and avoid them. According to the U.S. Department of

Agriculture, here is what you as a camper should know about each of these plants.

Poison Sumac—Sometimes known as swamp sumac, poison elder, poison ash, poison dogwood, and thunderwood, poison sumac grows as a coarse woody shrub or small tree. It never grows in the vinelike form of its poison-ivy relatives. The area of the United States where it is likely to be found is usually eastward toward the Atlantic coast from a line made up of eastern Minnesota, Illinois, Indiana, Kentucky, and Tennessee, down to southeastern Texas. This treelike shrub is usually found in swamps and bogs. The plants range in height from 5 or 6 feet to trees as high as 25 feet. Poison sumac leaves are divided into 7 to 13 leaflets, arranged in pairs with a single leaflet at the end of the midrib.

The leaflets are an elongated oval shape without teeth or serrations on the margins. Leaflets are 3 to 4 inches long and 1 to 2 inches wide, with a smooth velvetlike texture and bright-orange color when they first appear in spring. Later they become dark green and glossy on the upper surface, pale green on the lower, and have scarlet midribs. Early in fall, they turn to a brilliant red-orange or russet shade.

The small yellowish-green flowers are borne in clusters in slender stems arising from the axis of leaves along the smaller branches. The slender clusters of flowers are similar in general appearance to the poison-ivy flower, but they hang in much longer clusters. The flowers mature into ivory-white or green fruits resembling those of poison oak or poison ivy, except that they are usually less compact and hang in loose clusters that may be 10 to 12 inches long.

Many *nonpoisonous* sumacs are also found in swamps. These sumacs are easily distinguished from the poison variety. The nonpoisonous sumacs have red fruits and seed clusters, which always grow upward from the tip of the branches. The poisonous variety has fruits and seeds that hang down.

Common Poison Ivy—Some form of common poison ivy may be found in almost every part of the country, with the exception of the dry Southwest. The plant is known by many local names—poison ivy, three-leaf ivy, poison creeper, climbing sumac, poison oak, markweed, picry, and mercury.

Common poison ivy is most often found as a vine growing in woods and swamps, where it depends upon trees for support. Quite often, especially in a swamp, the vines of poison ivy will grow for many years, becoming several inches in diameter and quite woody.

When poison ivy becomes mixed with other vines, such as honeysuckle and greenbrier, it is difficult to detect except by the camper who has carefully trained himself in recognizing the plant.

Some other vines and young plants also resemble poison ivy in many respects. The Virginia creeper and some forms of the Boston ivy are often confused with it. The Virginia creeper can always be recognized by its five leaflets radiating from one point of attachment, as compared to the three leaflets of poison ivy arranged in the same manner. The Boston ivy with three leaflets is sometimes difficult to distinguish. However, not all the leaves on the Boston-ivy plant will be divided into three leaflets. The leaves of the common poison ivy are extremely variable, the three leaflets being the only constant character. It is impossible to describe the great

range of variation in the shape or lobing of the leaflets.
Most poison-ivy vines or shrubs produce some
flowers that are always in clusters arising on the side of
the stem immediately above a leaf. Frequently the
flowers do not develop or are abortive and produce no
fruit. When fruits do develop, they serve as a positive
way of identifying the plant. The berries are not easily
confused with the fruits of other plants. They are white
and look waxy. They have rather distinct lines marking
the outer surface, something like the segments in a
peeled orange. The fruit is especially helpful in identifying plants late in fall, in winter, and in early spring,
when the leaves are not present.

Oakleaf Poison Ivy—Of the several kinds of poison ivy,
the oakleaf form occurring in the eastern and southern
states is more distinctive than some other types. The
oakleaf poison ivy usually does not climb as a vine but
rather occurs as a low-growing shrub. The shrub's
rather slender branches often have a kind of downy
appearance. The leaflets occur in threes, as in other ivy,
but are lobed, somewhat on the general plan of some
oak leaves. The middle leaflet usually is lobed somewhat alike on both margins and very much resembles a
small oakleaf. The two lateral leaflets are often irregularly lobed.

The fruit of oakleaf poison ivy has the same general
appearance as the fruit of common poison ivy, although
the individual fruits and stems are often downy. Most
of the other forms have a waxy, smooth, cream-colored
fruit.

Poisoning—The skin irritant of poison ivy, poison oak, and poison sumac is the same toxic agent. It is a nonvolatile phenolic substance called urushiol and is found in all parts of the plant, including roots and fruit. It occurs in great abundance in the plant sap. The danger of poisoning is greatest in spring and summer when the sap is abundant, and it is least dangerous late in fall or in winter.

Poisoning is usually caused by contact with some part of the plant. A very small quantity of the poisonous substance can produce severe inflammation of the skin and can easily be transferred from one subject to another. Clothing may become contaminated. In fact, it is often a source of such prolonged infection that the victim's poisoning is likely to be judged as a case that's difficult to cure.

Hunting dogs frequently touch the plants and transmit the poison to unsuspecting persons. The poison may remain on the fur of animals for a considerable period after they have walked or run through poison-ivy plants. Smoke from burning plants will carry the toxin and has been reported to cause severe cases of poisoning. Cases of children being poisoned by eating the fruit have been reported.

Warning: there's no truth in the belief that eating a few leaves of these plants will develop immunity. It never should be attempted. No part of the plant should ever be taken internally. It is a violent irritant and poisonous to man. The time between contamination of the skin and the first symptoms varies greatly with individuals and, probably, with conditions. The first symptoms of itching or burning may develop in a few hours, or after 5 days, or maybe even longer. The itching sensation and subsequent inflammation, which usually develops into water blisters under the skin, may continue for several days from a single contamination. Persistence of symptoms over a long period is likely to be caused by new contacts with plants or with previously contaminated clothing or animals. Severe infection may produce more serious symptoms, which result in much pain through abscesses, enlarged glands, fever, or complicated constitutional malfunction. Secondary infections are always a possibility in any break in the skin, such as is produced by breaking large water blisters.

Treatment—Once you have been exposed to a member of the Rhus family, take a bath or shower and wash thoroughly with a strong, nonoily soap. Brown laundry soap works best. After the wash, swab the contacted skin with rubbing alcohol. If irritation appears on the skin, it can be reduced by using calamine lotion or Solarcaine. Avoid scratching the irritated skin with your fingernails; infection could be the result. If the case becomes painful, get medical attention at once.

9

Swamp Navigation

Navigation is a skill that is necessary in all swamp travels. Finding the way through extensive areas of swamps has always been a challenge to the wilderness traveler. Enough research has been done to prove that the ability to find your way is not instinctive. It's a skill that is learned.

The word *navigation* is frightening to many beginning swamp campers. For them, it creates images of sextants, chronometers, and other complicated instruments. But as any seasoned backpacker, hunter, fisherman, or trapper can testify, swamp navigation simply means having a working knowledge of a map and compass, and having the good sense to know when you need a guide.

Poor navigational skills can prevent you from enjoying your sport to the fullest. Several years ago, while I was working a deer hunt on the Suwanoochee Game Management Area in the flat swampy country of south Georgia, I noticed—as I had many times before—that a number of hunters were hunting within sight of their

Sometimes an experienced local guide is the best navigational technique you can have.

cars. Other staff members had noticed the same thing, so we decided to ask as many hunters as we could why they didn't venture further into the woods to better habitat. The results were unanimous: "I don't want to get lost."

There are many reasons to learn map-and-compass skills besides the considerable advantage of not getting lost. It is easy to return to that old tom you roosted last night if you recorded its location on the map by using compass bearings. That bluegill bed that you want to go back to can be found by using the same method. Many times I have used my compass and a simple map that I drew to find my way back to a line of scrapes a buck was working, to a white-oak grove the squirrels were cutting, or to a trap line that was in new territory.

The first step in learning map-and-compass navigation is to get a good compass. There are many good compasses on the market today. I find, however, that the Silva Safari best serves my purposes for swamp travel. After you buy your compass, you will want to read very carefully the instructions that come with it. (It is not the purpose of this book to teach elementary compass reading, but many good books are available that cover the subject.) These instructions will point out the basics for reading a compass:

1. The needle always points to magnetic north unless it is pulled off by some nearby metal object such as a knife, a nearby car, a belt buckle, and so on.

2. The compass dial is divided into 360°. When you line up the north end of the needle in your compass with the 360° line (usually marked with an N), your compass is in a reading position. In other words, it is as though you are standing in the center of the compass and from there anything in view may be lined up with a degree value. That line of direction is called a bearing.

Learning to set your compass up and read a bearing is simple, but it will take some practice.

The second step in learning map and compass navigation is to learn how to read a U.S. Geological Survey map.

It never ceases to amaze me how many sportsmen don't know where to get a topo map and don't understand how to read one. Almost all areas of the United States have been topographically mapped by the U.S. Geological Survey, a division of the Department of the Interior. These topographic maps have been described as a graphic representation of man-made and natural features of a part of the earth's surface, plotted to a definite scale. The distinguishing characteristic of these maps is that they show the shape and elevation of the terrain. They also show the location and shape of swamps; mountains; valleys; plains; streams; rivers; and works of man such as roads, buildings, and utility lines.

Topographical maps (or topo maps, as they are more frequently called) are made from a quadrangle unit of survey that is bound by parallels of latitude and meridians of longitude. The topo maps that are of the greatest assistance to sportsmen are quadrangles that cover 7½ minutes of latitude and longitude and are published at a scale of 1:24,000. In other words, 1 inch on the map equals 2,000 feet on the earth's surface. Each map is designated by the name of a city, town, community, or prominent natural feature within it. Each map has its name in bold letters at the lower right-hand corner. If the area you are interested in covers more than that one map, the names of adjoining maps will be found printed on the margins of the map you start with. Since the 7½-minute-series map covers only from 49 to 70 square miles, you may often need to get several adjoining maps in order to cover an entire hunting area or stream. Topo maps are printed with three basic colors—man-made features in black, water areas in blue, and relief features such as mountains and valleys in brown contour lines. The sportsman should always request topo maps with a woodland overprint— that is, all woodlands shown in green.

The process of ordering topographical maps is relatively simple. First write to the U.S. Geological Survey for an index of maps for your chosen state. Maps of areas east of the Mississippi River, including Minnesota, should be ordered from the Branch of Distribution, U.S. Geological Survey, 1200 South Eads Street, Arlington, Virginia 22202. Maps of areas west of the Mississippi River should be ordered from the Branch of Distribution, U.S. Geological Survey, Box 25276, Federal Center, Denver, Colorado 80225.

When you receive an index, find the swamp in which you are interested. It will be within one or more black squares, and a name is printed in each square—the name of a map. Write the appropriate U.S. Geological Survey office and ask for the maps you want by name, series, and state. For example, a map order may be: "Two copies of Wedgefield, 7½-minute series, South Carolina, with woodland overprint." The cost is $1.25 per map, payable by money order or check made out to U.S. Geological Survey.

Since topo maps are updated only every few years, you may need to add to your maps a few man-made features such as roads or towers. The date on which the map was surveyed is printed under the map name in the lower right-hand corner.

A topo map, like a compass, is not better or worse than the person using it. It behooves the sportsman to take the time to learn to read a topo map. The simplest way is to buy a map of an area near your home with which you are familiar. Take the map, and drive the roads. Relate the map symbols to on-the-ground, man-made, and natural features. Next, walk a distance cross-country, up a hill, and down into a valley. Study the contour lines on the map and relate them to the rise and fall of the land. Think of the contour line as an imaginary line on the ground which takes any shape necessary in order to maintain a constant elevation. As you study the contour lines, you'll notice that every fourth or fifth line; depending on the contour interval, will be a heavier brown line. Such a line is known as an index contour. Along this contour you will find the elevation printed at intervals. The elevation at any point can be determined by first finding an index contour line and then interpolating.

Let's take a specific example. Suppose your point on the map is two contour lines uphill from the index-contour line that's marked 100 feet. Suppose further that the contour interval (indicated at the bottom center of the map under the map's scale) is 10 feet. Then the elevation at your point is 120 feet.

As you learn to read the contour lines, you will notice that the closer they are together, the steeper the terrain will be; the farther apart they are, the gentler the terrain will be. Since most swamps are in flat terrain, the contour lines will be very wide apart, indicating few or no terrain features for help in navigation.

Also learn to use your map's scale. It will help you to estimate the distance and the travel time to hunting, fishing, or camping areas. On the 7½-minute-series topo map, each 2⅝ inches equals 1 mile.

The map and compass are basic for all swamp navigation. But you should also be aware that various types of swamps require navigational techniques that are unusually appropriate to the swamp's character. Let's look at a few of these techniques.

The river-bottom swamp (or flood plain, as it is often called) can be traveled by boat or during dry periods by walking. If it is to be traveled by boat, the river should be the main route of travel. If the river bottom is flooded, then side trips may be made from the river.

The first step in a trip of this type is to sit down with someone who is familiar with the swamp river and get him to show you the best course on a topo map. Many times a swamp river will meander, offering several channels from which the boat user must choose one. If you choose the wrong one, it can mean a return trip upstream for another selection.

You'll be able to choose the right channel instead of the wrong one if you've taken the trouble to get accurate information marked on your topographical map beforehand. Credit: Georgia Industry & Trade.

Be sure to consider the water level. Areas that are easily accessible during high water may be difficult or impossible to reach during times of low water.

Most local people know the best channel. Find out how long it takes to float a stretch of river and what obstacles, such as fallen trees, can be expected. Many times a slow-moving, log-choked swamp river can require a lot of time to float just 1 mile. Many swamp travelers have stayed in a swamp several days longer than they'd planned. The reason? Miscalculating their speed of travel.

Also find out good campsite locations before making your trip. Campsites that are good during periods of low water may be underwater during periods of high water. On the other hand, good campsites during high water may be inaccessible during low water. Mark these campsites on your topo map.

Navigating down a river is relatively easy if you know the proper channels to follow. The more difficult navigating starts when you want to boat or canoe into the flooded river swamps adjacent to the main river. Here the approach most often used is the *baseline method* of navigation.

You leave the main river channel (baseline) at a known point—your camp (see accompanying sketch). You decide to fish the river swamp to the west, roughly following a bearing of 260°. You have fished for 2 miles, wandering to the right and to the left of your intended route because of logs, trees, and other obstacles. You have not kept track of these slight changes in direction.

Then you're ready to return to camp. You know the river (baseline) is to the east. You also know that a reverse bearing of 80° (figured by subtracting 180° from the 260° bearing you came in on) will put you back on the river near your camp. However, there is a good possibility you will hit the river and not know whether to go upstream or down. To make certain

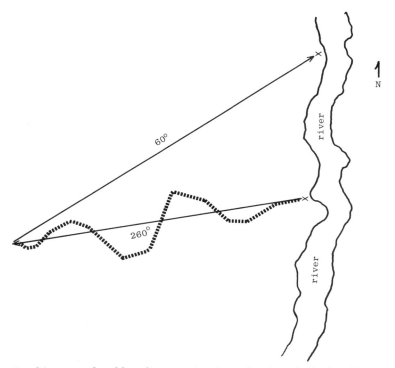

In this example of baseline navigation, the river is the baseline.

which side of camp you will be on, you should strongly favor a point too far upstream of your 80° return route. For instance, you could return on a 60° bearing. Then when you came to the river you would know you should go downstream. A few extra strokes of the paddle, but it is much better than paddling in the wrong direction.

If you're backpacking into a river swamp during a dry period of the year, this same method will work, provided you use a logging road or some similar feature as your baseline. There's no doubt that some of the best hunting in North America is in river-bottom swamps, but such places are among the easiest in which to get lost. Because the terrain is so flat, a topo map is often of little use.

In this situation, your compass becomes very important. Your understanding of baseline navigation can make a day in the swamp much more enjoyable. Incidentally, the ice in many northern swamps can be traveled upon during the winter, and the baseline method works well under these conditions, too.

The vast, wet swamps such as the Dismal, Okefenokee, and Everglades offer the swamp traveler a different challenge. Here navigation is reduced to following existing canals and trails. You can try it on your own, if you're capable, or go with a guide. To venture off these marked waterways would be asking for trouble. Getting from one point to another without using existing trails is generally impossible because of the thick growth on the swamp floor. The use of existing trails is not an insult to your woodsmanship but a wise decision that will assure your enjoyment of your swamp trip.

Other vast swamps such as the Big Thicket of Texas and the Atchafalya of Louisiana require the services of a local guide for newcomers. It has been said that the best navigational skill is to know when you need a guide. These and other large swamps that do not have a trail or marked waterway system are no place for you to practice amateur navigational skills. After all, you are in the swamp to enjoy camping, hunting, and fishing, not to practice survival. Unlike being lost on dry land, if you get lost in a swamp, chances are you can't walk out and you can't paddle in a straight line. Use a local guide and concentrate on your sporting activities.

Two additional methods you may want to consider

are: (1) the bearing-and-distance method, and (2) the trial-and-error method.

• The bearing-and-distance method works well in swamps that are not thickly vegetated and where terrain features can be spotted at a distance. Here is an example of how it works.

Someone has marked a good hunting campsite for you on a topo map. In the comfort of your dining room, take your map and compass and line up North. With a straight edge, line up the first leg of the trip, say from where you will park your car on the road to the first well-defined landmark—perhaps a microwave relay tower. Scale measure the distance to this landmark, and compute the bearing to it and the return bearing from it. Record this information in pencil on your map or on a separate sheet. Do the same thing with each additional leg of the trip. When you finish this job, your route should be marked on the map and you should have enough information to travel to and from the campsite.

EXAMPLE:

	Distance	Bearing Out	Return Bearing
Car to relay tower	1 mile	355°	175°
Tower to island	1 mile	55°	235°
Island to campsite	.5 mile	38°	218°

In order to use this method, you'll need some practice in judging the distance you walk or paddle. But by carefully following bearings and watching landmarks, you'll find it relatively simple to make a round trip and stay on course. Many times I have marked my trip in with white surveyor's tape and collected it on the

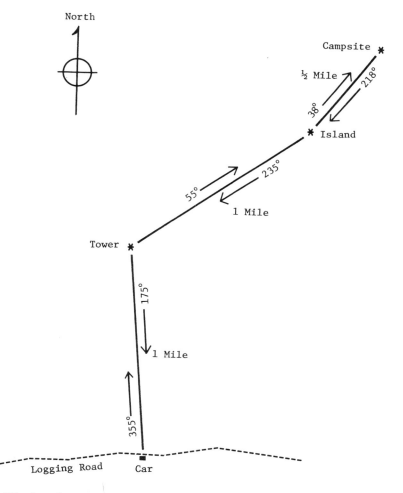

North

Campsite ✳

½ Mile

38°   218°

✳ Island

55°   235°

1 Mile

Tower ✳

175°

1 Mile

355°

Logging Road   Car

The bearing-and-distance method is something you can use at home to plot simultaneously both your route in and your return.

way out. Not like Daniel Boone, I admit, but I got out much quicker than I otherwise would have.

• The trial-and-error method simply involves using white-plastic surveyor's marking tape and roughly following a compass course to your destination. When you come to a dead end, you backtrack, collecting the strips of tape as you go, and then try another route. When you finally reach your destination, you get out your map for the return trip and mark your newfound route. Be sure to collect the tape on the way out.

A navigational technique used by fishermen on swamp lakes to mark good fishing spots is known as resection. Here is how you can use it (see accompanying sketch.)

Let's say you're on a swamp lake for the first time and have found a bluegill bed. You want to fish the bed again tomorrow. Choose two features that you think you can find again (we'll call them A and B). Each must be identifiable on your map as well as on the ground. With your compass, read the bearing from the bluegill bed to each of these points. Then compute their reverse bearings by adding 180° (or if the bearing is greater than 180, by subtracting 180). These will be the bearings from the features to the bluegill bed. Place the compass at feature A on your map, and draw a line along its reverse bearing. Do the same at feature B on the map. Your bluegill bed is where the two lines cross.

Navigating across swamps is complicated even for well-trained navigators. Swamp maps generally lack detail; the swamps themselves lack prominent terrain features; and you run into such problems as the dense undergrowth, the sudden shallowness or lack of water for the boater, or the sudden wetness for the hiker.

The best navigational skill in any swamp is the familiarity that comes with many days and nights of

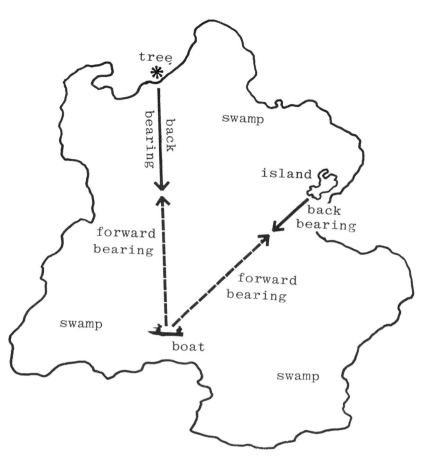

A navigational technique known technically as resection is a fairly simple way to find your way back another day to a productive fishing spot.

experience in that swamp. The difficulty of getting conventional navigational techniques to work in swamps is the chief factor in our swamps' being one of our last truly wild spots left to explore. As mentioned before, the best navigational technique for a large unfamiliar swamp is a guide who knows the area.

10

Swamp Survival

EXPECT THE UNEXPECTED

A swamp is perhaps the easiest place in North America for you to suddenly need survival skills. Basically, there are three swamp predicaments that are considered survival situations.

• With all the debris in the water, it is easy to foul an outboard motor or to puncture a canoe; or in the always unpredictable mud, a four-wheel drive vehicle can become hopelessly stuck.

• The next survival situation is simply that you get lost. The swamp is flat, and everything looks alike on a gray day. Directions are impossible to decipher.

• The third survival situation is that you or a partner get sick or injured and can't get help.

Strandings are often difficult to avoid. But a top priority of yours should always be to let someone know where you're going camping and when you plan to return. Always keep your equipment in good repair, and have a backup system or at least a repair kit. Avoid weather that could get you into trouble, and avoid areas from which your return may be impossible. In other words, use some common sense.

A good investment in a boat or backcountry vehicle is a C.B. (citizens band) radio. C.B. radios are used almost everywhere you go these days; therefore someone should hear your distress signal. In a stranding, you're usually better off to stay with the vehicle rather than to try walking out at night or during a storm. Remember, a vehicle, boat, or canoe is easier to spot from the air than an individual.

The most frequent cause of a swamp survival situation is that somebody gets lost. For most people, getting lost is a sobering 2- or 3-hour experience. For others, the experience is fatal.

Elton Harris walked out of his Alabama yard with his three beagles for an afternoon rabbit hunt. He did not plan to get lost, so he carried no matches or survival gear. When darkness came, Harris suddenly realized he was lost. The mercury plunged to 10°F., and he burrowed down into leaves in a small cave with his three dogs. After a long icy night, Harris tried to get up and couldn't. His wet pants and boots were frozen. After much effort he got his legs working and found his way back home. The warmth from his dogs probably saved his life.

Getting lost is easy, and it happens at one time or another to most active outdoorsmen. Getting found, however, is not so easy.

Very few sportsmen carry a compass and a map of the area in which they plan to travel, especially in areas they go to regularly. A map and compass plus the skill to use them and the respect of the unknown that makes you use them can keep you "found" all your days afield. But, a map and compass that you are not sure how to read are virtually useless. So are a map and compass that are never referred to.

A good course in orienteering is recommended for anyone who plans to enjoy the outdoors. Anybody who has hunted squirrels in a flatwoods on a gray overcast day knows that it takes more than a so-called sense of direction to get back to where you started.

Another reason that many people get lost is their lack of attention to their surroundings. I firmly believe that no one is born with a sense of direction. Accurate backcountry travel is a skill that is learned, and the most important part of the skill is to keep your eyes open—basic observation. In our day-to-day life, we unconsciously use landmarks around our home town all the time. But in an unknown area we must pay attention to landmarks, know how they look in all directions, and record them in our minds. As a small boy, I was told by my dad, a master outdoorsman, to look backward periodically so that I could recognize the trail and landmarks on the way out. That teaching is still with me. I do it now almost without thinking.

A classic example of not recording landmarks is the case of one lost bowhunter I helped find. He had gone from his camp into his hunting area using his compass. Then he'd set up his tree stand and got comfortable for a day of waiting.

That afternoon he hit a deer. After a few minutes of waiting, the hunter left his tree stand. He also left his day pack and coat behind so that he could comfortably trail the wounded deer.

The deer, not badly hit, crossed two beaver swamps. The bowhunter lost the deer's trail in the second swamp and suddenly realized he had not paid attention to landmarks while following the deer. His compass and map were in his coat, and so were his matches. It was getting dark.

We found that hunter the next morning in a state of panic. He had a case of hypothermia and was scratched and torn from a night of running.

Tracking wounded game is going to take you to an unknown destination. Be prepared! You will have to come back, so be observant. Remember landmarks. Carry your map, compass, and survival basics with you.

The sudden accident often puts outdoorsmen into a survival situation. Several years ago, I was hunting with a 300-pound sportsman in the coastal swamps of Virginia. Richard had walked some 3 miles from our camp and was standing on a slick log when a deer jumped up behind him. Turning to look, he lost his balance and took a hard fall that shattered his leg. Unable to move, he had to make a survival camp until we found him.

A broken leg or legs in a swamp can put you in a survival situation when you least expect it. I know of two cases where falls from tree stands immobilized hunters so that the survival camp became a must.

There are two rules you should follow to prevent this type situation.

• Number one, don't go into a swamp alone. Be sure to let your pardner know generally where you plan to hunt, fish, or hike, and when you plan to get back. If Richard hadn't told us where his 3-mile hunt was going to take place and when he expected to get back to camp, it could have taken us days to find him.

• Rule number two is to always let your people at home, or the motel where you're staying, know where you're going and when you plan to return. An extra precaution is to leave a note on the windshield of your car stating who you are, the direction you are walking, and when you plan to return.

These rules properly followed can't prevent you

from having an immobilizing accident, but they can cut down on the number of hours you must go through your ordeal.

Despite all precautions, many of us will sooner or later need to be able to take care of ourselves in the backcountry until help comes.

The best survival plan must be based on the priorities that maintain life, and the best way to remember this is to learn the "rule of threes." You can live 3 weeks or more without food, 3 days without water, 3 hours without protection in hostile weather, and 3 minutes without air.

SKILLS TO LIVE

Each year hundreds of outdoorsmen are suddenly shocked into the reality that even they can get lost, stranded, weathered-in, or immobilized by injury. At that point they must put to work their "skills to live."

If you've taken the time to learn survival skills and to prepare yourself for the unexpected, then your situation will be one of adventure and challenge rather than an ordeal or perhaps tragedy.

The first step toward survival is to always let someone know where you are going into a swamp and when you expect to return. If you get into trouble, authorities will soon be notified and they will know the right area in which to begin the search.

Let's assume it is a nice spring day and you have walked 2 miles out of camp in order to fish a remote beaver swamp. Late in the afternoon the sky begins to cloud up, and you decide to head for camp. On the way out you lose the trail. Suddenly you realize that you're lost. Night is rapidly approaching. What do you do?

The most important survival skill in such a situation is your ability to admit that you really are lost. With this fact accepted, stop, sit down, and think. Convince yourself to avoid panic and to stay calm. Accept the challenge, and prepare to make the best of your adventure. If you told friends or family at home or at camp where you were going and when you planned to return, chances are someone will begin looking for you soon after dark. In fact, most lost people are found within a few hours after they are reported missing. Even in the more remote swamps of the United States, 99 percent of the lost people are found within 72 hours.

Once you get over the initial shock of realizing that you are lost, look around you and evaluate your situation.

Since people will be looking for you soon, your first concern should probably be preparing to let people know where you are. In our assumed lost case, as in most lost cases, a fire is the best signal device. At night it can be seen for miles from the air and for a fair distance on the ground. Before dark, the smoke can be seen from the air as well as from forest-fire towers, which watch over many of the nation's swamps. A fire does more than serve as a good signal. It also keeps you warm, gives you a somewhat reassuring feeling, and can be used for cooking. More about fires later.

Other signal devices that you may want to consider include a whistle. The sound of a whistle can be heard much farther than the human voice and will last long after a shouting person becomes hoarse. A small mirror or shiny object can be seen for miles from an airplane during the day. A plane can also spot a blaze-orange vest, a white T-shirt, or even light-colored skin if the lost person is in an open area.

Small serial flares are effective for night use, and

The reflection from a small mirror or other shiny object can be seen for miles from a plane or helicopter. All pilots know that a large "X" made from logs, rocks, or other material is a signal for help.

Searcher in a plane or helicopter is more likely to spot victim who presents areas of light-colored skin or clothing and moves them around as search craft approaches.

blaze-orange smoke signals are helpful for day use. These handy devices are available from Survival Systems, Inc., 1830 S. Baker Avenue, Ontario, California 91761.

If all else fails, find an opening in the swamp and make a large "X" with logs, rocks, or whatever else is available. All airplane pilots know the X is a signal for help.

Using some combination of any or all of these signals is a first step toward being found.

A word of caution: many survival books suggest firing three evenly spaced shots as a lost signal. It doesn't work. During hunting season, three shots are heard all the time. Recently, for instance, I was hunting with outdoor writer Tom Gresham when he got his four-wheel-drive vehicle hopelessly stuck far back in a swamp. Several times he fired three shots, and none of our hunting party paid any attention. Tom, after a long, cold walk, told us in person about his problem. The only time three shots might work is when you know a search party is in the area. Three shots otherwise are meaningless.

Let's return to our lost situation. You realize you're lost, you've calmed down, and you've wisely decided to wait for rescue. You find a nearby opening in the swamp, where our signals can be seen from the air, and you take out your waterproof match container and build a fire. Sounds easy doesn't it? What if you didn't have matches? What if you didn't know how to properly build a fire? An inexperienced person might say you can always build a fire with flint and steel or by making a fire drill. The same greenhorn might also say that anybody can build a fire. How wrong he'd be!

Except for a handful of experts, few among us can start a fire without matches. Despite what many survival books tell you, there is *no substitute for dry matches in a survival situation.* Make it a practice to carry a waterproof match container with you at all times in the backcountry.

Now for the common misconception that most outdoorsmen with matches can build a fire. Recently I was talking with a veteran search-and-rescue official who pointed out that each year he finds many lost outdoorsmen who are cold and without fire. "Most of them had matches," he told me, "but they used them up just trying to get a fire started."

Take the time to learn an old Boy Scout skill: build a fire with just one match. Learn what makes good tinder—a bird nest, steel wool (yes, steel wool), bark from a river birch tree, pine lighter (found on the ground around old pine stumps), or cedar bark. Don't assume you know this skill. Go out, find the materials, and use them to build a fire.

In a damp situation, don't forget that dead standing trees and their branches are usually drier than downed stuff. Dead lower branches of growing evergreen trees also tend to be dry. Take the time now to become a fire-building expert. This know-how may save your life. Also remember that in a swamp situation, a fire may be necessary to discourage hordes of mosquitoes.

Not long ago, two young men were exploring the Pearl River Swamp in Mississippi when night caught them far from camp. When darkness halted them, they pulled up on a dry island to spend the night. After striking all their matches in a futile sequence of attempting to get a fire going, the two lay on the ground to try escaping the hundreds of hungry mosquitoes that fed on their blood. The next morning the two men staggered into camp bitten to the point of needing hospitalization. Had they gotten a fire going and kept enough green material on it to create a thick smoke, their ordeal would not have been half so bad.

After you have a fire going, what next? You recall that when you got lost, night was approaching and the sky was cloudy. Your next consideration should be shelter. On a cold winter's evening, shelter is a must. The easiest shelter to make is a lean-to, especially if you have a small Space brand blanket. If you don't have one of these small blankets that fold to the size of a cigarette pack, consider roofing your lean-to with pine needles, loose bark, or whatever you can find. Use your imagination. To keep your mind occupied and off your predicament, see how good a shelter you can make.

I recall fondly one hunter I helped find several years ago in Georgia. He had been lost for 2 days. When we found him, he had almost established a homestead. In fact, he had built himself such a cozy camp that we used it for an overnight rest before packing out. On the way out, he told us his experience had been a ball.

Other quick shelters can be made from blown-down trees and overturned canoes. Use due caution with fire, and don't camp with a den of cottonmouths. Common sense and a little ingenuity can do a lot to help you build an adequate shelter. Many times a shelter is not necessary, but you be the judge.

Many outdoorsmen think that food and water are the most important needs in a survival situation. Far from it. It has been proven many times that most people can live 3 days without water and easily 3 weeks or more without food. So don't panic and think you might die from the lack of food or water the first night. Odds are great that you'll be found long before any great need for either occurs.

If you travel into extremely remote country where rescue might be longer in coming, you may want to

In situations that call for inclusion of a survival gun in your swamp-camping equipment, the author prefers this 2½-pound rifle.

pack a survival gun for possible food gathering. Since my work involves deep backcountry travel by canoe, horse, four-wheel-drive vehicle, and backpack, I make it a practice to carry a survival gun.

After trying several handguns, I have decided that the best survival gun is the Charter Arms AR-7 Explorer .22 rifle. This little 2½-pound rifle has five simple elements, all of which store neatly in the floating stock. I have found the rifle highly accurate. It has come in handy many times for everything from eliminating a rabid fox to supplementing the camp stew with a rabbit. If ever I get lost in a long-term situation, I feel confident that the AR-7 would be a welcome addition to my survival kit. If you would feel more comfortable with a gun as part of your survival gear— whether for protection, food gathering, or whatever— in my opinion the AR-7 is the best choice.

As insurance for any outdoorsman, it's hard to beat a survival kit that he knows how to use. I know of a canoeist who carried a survival kit for years. When he finally lost his canoe in a set of rapids in a remote area, he almost died because he panicked and didn't know how to use the kit's ingredients.

For your boat, plane, family car, hunting vehicle, or any other type vehicle, I recommend the MK-1 Survival Kit put out by Survival Systems, Inc. It has everything you need to survive almost any situation. In fact, you could probably homestead the "back forty" with it.

Almost all seasoned backcountry travelers carry a small survival kit with them at all times. For the past 15 years I have been carrying one that I've used many times. Not only is it my survival kit, but it also serves as a readily available first-aid kit.

In it are the items necessary for signalling, shelter, fire making, navigation, and first aid. It weighs 2 pounds and fits easily on my belt. The kit is made up of the following items.

1. The kit bag itself is an army-surplus individual first-aid pouch. It is sturdy and fits the belt easily. Also, its small size allows it to fit into a day pack, backpack, vehicle glove compartment, or a tackle box.

2. The orange smoke signal from Survival Systems, Inc. is an excellent daytime signal device to use in conjunction with ground-to-air signals.

3. The wire saw, which coils up to store easily, can be used to cut poles for shelter, for firewood, or for helping to quarter big-game carcasses.

4. Many survival stories are told of hunters who reached a pay phone on a parkway or at a closed lodge and had no change for a call. Carry enough change for a call.

5. A coil of 20-pound-test fishing line can be used for shelter making, mending clothes, and making snares, as well as for fishing.

6. The folded Space brand emergency blanket is the size of a cigarette pack, but when open it can be made into a lean-to or used as a blanket to reflect up to 90 percent of your body heat.

7. Aspirin to ease pain.

8. Band-Aids.

9. Police whistle for signaling.

10. A candle stub (an excellent fire-starter).

11. A scout-type pocket knife, which has many uses in the survival camp.

12. Antiseptic for scratches and wounds.

13. Signal mirror. It can be spotted for miles by search planes and forest-fire towers.

14. Beef broth has some food value and makes wild food dishes taste much better.

This is the survival kit developed and carried by the author. It consists of: 1) the kit bag, 2) orange smoke signal, 3) wire saw, 4) coins for phone, 5) fishing line, 6) Space brand emergency blanket, 7) aspirin, 8) Band-Aids, 9) whistle, 10) candle stub, 11) pocket knife, 12) antiseptic, 13) signal mirror, 14) dehydrated beef broth, 15) survival manual, 16) waterproof matches, 17) water-purification tablets, 18) "tackle box," 19) tweezers, 20) lip balm, 21) Metal Match, 22) steel wool, and 23) backup compass.

When he's in the swamp on a hunting trip, as shown here, on a fishing trip, or for some other reason, the author carries his lightweight survival kit in its kit bag on his belt.

15. The Wallet Survival Guide serves as a survival manual. From Wallet Survival Guide, P.O. Box 2947, Everett, WA 98203.

16. Waterproof matches in waterproof match safe.

17. Water-purification tablets.

18. A "tackle box" can be made by taking a small plastic bottle and winding several feet of 6-pound-test fishing line around it. Hold the line in place with tape. Into the bottle put several small fishhooks, split-shot, a small bluegill popping bug, and a small dry fly. Think small, as it is usually easier to catch small fish. (The food requirement during survival situations is less than most people think.)

19. Tweezers for removing splinters and ticks.

20. Lip protection from wind and sun.

21. Metal Match, which can be used as a backup fire-starter.

22. Size 000 steel wool. It's good when used with the metal match to get tinder started. One spark in the loose steel wool produces a hot glow that will start dry tinder. *Steel wool works even when wet.*

23. A backup compass. You should carry your primary compass on your person.

Remember: survival kits alone won't save your life; a kit plus survival skills will. Start preparing now for when you get lost or stranded. Learn the skills to live.

Someone once said that "lost" meant Lean on Survival Training. Survival preparedness should be a part of every swamp traveler's training. If we are conditioned to "expect the unexpected," then our days afield will be much more enjoyable.

WHEN ONE OF YOUR GROUP IS MISSING

A growing number of sportsmen are taking survival training and know what to do when they themselves are stranded or lost. Very few sportsmen, however, consider what they would do if a member of their group failed to return to camp at the end of the day.

I have a friend who was hunting deer with a group in a large swamp in the panhandle of Florida. One night a hunter failed to show up for supper. No one knew where he had hunted that day, so two of the group took flashlights and went into the swamp in different directions. Three other members of the group got into their trucks and started running up and down logging roads blowing their horns.

Around 2 a.m., someone went into town and got the local rescue squad, and by early sunrise they had found the lost hunter.

He had a complaint. Every time he had started toward the sound of a truck horn, it would move. He had spent the night unafraid, but he got worn out from chasing the ever-moving horns. As the hunters sat around camp eating breakfast and reliving the long night, someone suddenly realized that one of the two searchers who had gone into the swamp the night before with flashlights had not returned. Another search was under way. By late afternoon, the second man was found. He was in a state of total panic. Rather than hunt, the hunters spent the next 2 days in camp resting up for the trip home.

Those campers had never considered that such a thing could happen to them. When it did, they were unprepared. They acted out of panic, endangering the lost hunter as well as themselves.

Before you go on any swamp trip, recognize that a swamp is one of the easiest places on earth to get lost. Point out that fact to the other members of your group, and have a plan for keeping track of each other. Also have a plan for what to do if a member is suddenly missing. Make sure everyone understands the plan.

Each year I hunt deer with an experienced group of sportsmen from Birmingham, Alabama. They camp and hunt the Sipsey River Swamp in west-central Alabama. One of the first rules a newcomer learns upon coming into the camp is that they have a map of the swamp posted on a board and that each hunter, before leaving camp, must mark where he will hunt and when he plans to return. If the hunter changes locations, he must return to camp and change the map. This well-run camp has never had anyone lost for longer than an hour. A bonus of this system is that it keeps one hunter from accidentally spoiling the hunting of another.

It's a good rule for every swamp traveler to carry a police whistle. It makes locating him much faster. The sound of a whistle carries a long way in a swamp.

When you work out a search plan with your group, stress how important it is for the lost person to stay put until contact is made. Have a prearranged set of signals. Don't do as the Florida group did and blow horns as you drive around. If you have a vehicle nearby, blow the horn but keep the vehicle in one place.

If you or any of your swamp companions have medical problems, see to it that the situation is common knowledge. If a member of your group has a heart problem, fainting spells, or the like, make sure that he has a "buddy" to accompany him. There is nothing more discouraging for searchers than to go into a camp that has lost a hunter or fisherman and hear that he is alone and has a medical problem. Too many times the story has a sad ending, which a little forethought could have prevented.

Perhaps the most crucial time during a lost-person situation is when you realize that somebody is late coming into camp and you get no answers to your signals. Don't panic.

First, find out where the person was last known to be. Set up watch there. Next, send someone to notify the local sheriff's office, ranger station, or fish-and-wildlife station. Always know how to reach the appropriate authorities before you need them. Make this a part of your trip plan. While someone is going for professional search-and-rescue help, keep your group together and keep signalling at the watch point. Be alert for first replies to your signals. Don't organize your own "piece-meal" search. Most of the time this only adds to the problem. Let the professionals organize the search.

Every lost-person situation differs to some degree from others, but usually these basic rules will assure a speedy and orderly swamp rescue. If the lost person is properly prepared, the whole event will be over in no time.

11

Planning a Trip

Some of the most valuable time spent on any outdoor trip is the time you spend planning and preparing. A fast, unplanned trip can be a miserable failure in many ways. You throw into the car a hodge-podge of equipment and drive for miles without knowing if the hunting or fishing regulations have changed, if the swamp is still owned or controlled by the same people, or what the weather forecast is. The items you forget will usually cost more on the road—if you can find them. Trips that are thrown together turn out to be expensive, not so much fun, and often downright dangerous.

Planning an outdoor trip should be, and usually is, an enjoyable part of the experience. The nights of studying maps on the kitchen table, sessions in the garage checking gear to make sure you have what you need and that it works properly, phone conversations with local authorities to learn the conditions at the swamp, and finally the time spent carefully packing the car with your gear are all part of the excitement that makes swamp camping such a pleasurable adventure. Not only that, planning also saves you time and money.

Here are some examples of how planning will pay off for you.

SELECTING THE RIGHT AREA FOR YOUR PURPOSE

Nothing can be more disheartening than to drive for a day to reach a swamp and find that it is almost dry, or the deer season is temporarily closed, or the area requires a special permit from the nonresident owner. Such problems can be avoided.

The best method to use in selecting an area is to talk to reliable people who have been to various areas. Other sportsmen are always good for opinions of outdoor areas. They see a swamp through the eyes of a hunter or fisherman and can give you the benefit of their experience. It's a wise practice to spend some time on the phone with local authorities who have the responsibility of managing the swamp you're considering. If the swamp is in a state game-management area, call the local conservation officer. If the swamp is part of a federal wildlife refuge, then call the refuge manager's office. Maybe it's the property of a timber or pulp-and-paper company. If so, call their chief forester or wildlife biologist. If it's privately owned, find the owner.

Once you have found the right person, ask the right questions. Is the area open for your intended use? Is camping permitted? What are the game and fish conditions? What are the camping conditions? What is the best time of the year, lure, method, and so on? Have your questions written down beforehand in a logical form so that you can get the answers without taking too much of the other person's time.

Once you have selected a swamp, your next task is to get some good maps of the area. The chapter on swamp navigation has instructions on how to order U.S. Geological Survey topographical maps. These maps are a valuable aid in planning any outdoor trip. You will also want to find out if other maps are available. Many times swamps in state wildlife-management areas, federal wildlife refuges, state parks, national forests, national parks, and timber-company management areas will have special maps that are helpful in trip planning.

When you have a good map or set of maps, keep your notes on the map. Mark good campsites, fishing and hunting hotspots, safe drinking water, and so on. It's easy to forget this information, but on a map it will last.

Be sure you get permission to use the swamp. If it is privately owned, get written permission that spells out what your rights are. For instance, can you camp, hunt, and fish? Make sure the dates of the trip are included and that the owner or his authorized agent has signed the permission. If the swamp is on government land, get whatever permit is required. Again, make sure that you are allowed to do what you want and when you want to do it. A fishing permit doesn't give you the right to camp or hunt. Make sure you are selecting a swamp in which you can do what you plan. An error can put you in violation of the law.

Find out what you must do in order to get hunting or fishing licenses, fire permits, camping permits, special stamps, and such. Also get season dates, bag limits, shooting or fishing hours, and any other special instructions.

The Okefenokee National Wildlife Refuge is a good example. You can camp only on the canoe trails in the swamp and only at designated camping shelters. A special camping permit is required, and you may stay at the campsite for only a designated time. (This regulation is to assure that overcrowding will not occur and that campers will get a true swamp wilderness experience.) Fishing in the refuge requires a Georgia fishing license. Hunting or firearms are not permitted. Georgia state creel limits are enforced, and fishing is permitted only during daylight hours.

If sportsmen unfamiliar with these regulations went to the Okefenokee and put in without checking, they could very easily violate every one of these rules. Check out such details before you leave home. It could save you a long trip for nothing, a lot of embarrassment, or both.

Until you know a swamp well yourself, you'd be wise to hire a reputable local guide. Good swamp guides rarely can be booked on short notice. Those that can may not be of the quality you want. So make arrangements for your guide or outfitter well in advance, and take the trouble to get references and check them out. Two days into the heart of a swamp is no time to learn that your guide is a drunk who brought only beans and whiskey to feed you. Also arrange well in advance for any rental gear you may be depending upon, such as boats or canoes, and secure them with a deposit.

If you're taking a float trip down a swamp river, you'll want to arrange, well in advance, to have someone meet you downriver at a designated pickup point. I have found that for a small fee the proprietors of reputable service stations in nearby towns will usually drop you off at the start, securely store your car, and pick you up at the end. This arrangement is much better than leaving cars along the river, where they could be vandalized or stolen. And if you don't show up at the designated time, you have a local person who can notify the authorities.

SELECTING THE RIGHT EQUIPMENT FOR THE ACTIVITY

I was once on a deer hunt at a camp deep in a swamp of the Ohio River flood plain. The camp rules were that you could bring only one gun, and it had to be a shotgun. Late the night before the opening day of a deer hunt, an invited guest from New York arrived. Everyone was amazed to see that he had brought a .270 rifle. He hadn't bothered to read the camp rules, which had been sent to him earlier.

That hunter paced the camphouse floor for 2 days waiting for someone to bag a deer so that he could borrow a gun and hunt. He also became the camp cook since he had more free time than the rest of us. It pays to research your sport and the area you plan to visit so that you will have the right equipment.

When you're setting up your trip, find out the local conditions that could influence your visit. Is this the worst summer in history for mosquitoes in your chosen swamp? If so, you will want to take along an extra supply of repellent, check the netting of your tent for rips, and perhaps pack a mosquito head net. If the water level of the swamp is lower than usual and wading is a must, then an extra pair of jungle boots, pants, and socks will be necessary.

I know of a camper who drove 500 miles, pulling his shiny new bass boat to a swamp in Florida only to learn on arrival that the shallow water would not take a motor or a large boat.

On one trip I saw an unfortunate camper who

brought a homemade hammock. On that swamp-river float trip, the only good campsites were on treeless sandbars. That man had to set up camp each night back in the wet mosquito-infested woods while his campmates slept comfortably on breezy sandbars. He hadn't checked to see what the local conditions were when he was planning the trip.

Other points that should always be researched are the best methods of hunting or fishing the area. When I was guiding in south Georgia, it always caught me off guard to see a fisherman step off the plane with his Abercrombie & Fitch trout-fishing tackle and clothing. He hadn't taken the time to read the material I'd sent. I'd told him we would be fishing in swamps from canoes, and that heavy spinning tackle was required. We usually lost half a day reoutfitting such dudes.

You pay good money and spend valuable time to have what you hope will be a successful trip. Improve your odds by learning how the local people hunt or fish the swamp, and try to adapt to these methods. Most of the time they work.

Weather conditions should have a strong influence on your choice of camping equipment. A check of the recent weather conditions at the swamp is always in order. During hunting season, the snow may be deeper than you're prepared to tackle. Or maybe you were preparing for snow and it's unseasonably warm. Perhaps heavier-than-usual rains have made getting to the swamp a job for a four-wheel-drive vehicle and your family car would be useless. Maybe you were planning to float a swamp river and camp on sandbars, but the rains have the river rising and the sandbars will soon be underwater. See what the weather has been, and by all means see what the weather forecasts are for the time of your trip. Weather surprises can be dangerous, especially if you lack the right equipment. Plan your gear around sound weather advice. Then remember to keep an eye on the sky and use common sense.

Once you have selected the right equipment, take the time to pack it correctly. I once packed my backpack in a rush and had a boat drop me off a 2-day hike from my truck. That night when I was setting up camp, I discovered that my gas-stove cap was not tight and the fuel had dripped onto my food supply. I had to resort to wild foods. I'd been a sloppy packer, and it had cost me.

Once when I was guiding a group of college professors on a swamp crossing, one of these scholars packed a leaky water jug in the bag with our toilet paper. It made an interesting combination.

A friend of mine packed his gear in the trunk of his car for a deer-hunting trip to a remote swamp. After driving 40 bumpy miles, he opened the trunk to set up camp. The trunk was filled with the aroma of insect repellent. He had rushed his packing and had set an ice chest on the business end of the aerosol repellent can. He told me he didn't see any deer but the mosquitoes didn't bother him. His bowhunting equipment still smells of "Off" repellent.

Many campers have the right equipment but pack it wrong. Some examples are funny; many others are serious. A broken lantern, snapped fishing rod, or torn tent can suddenly turn an enjoyable trip into a headache. The old saying, "Anthing worth doing is worth doing right," is especially true when you are packing for your comfort, safety, and enjoyment in a remote swamp.

LAST-MINUTE DETAILS THAT
MAKE OR BREAK A TRIP

There are several details that require a little extra thought when you're planning a swamp-camping trip. Medication and special health needs are at the top of the list. I once had to rush a diabetic out of a swamp because he had forgotten his insulin. Anyone who requires medication should always make that his foremost concern.

Other things that people often forget are motorboat fuel, licenses and permits, and tent poles (my favorite item to forget). People too often leave their fish bait at home in the refrigerator or their ammunition in the storage room.

Things that aren't necessarily associated with camping should also be remembered, such as stopping the mail, milk and newspaper deliveries, and arranging the dog's care.

I was guiding a trip down the Suwanee River for a family once, and the wife decided the first night she had left her kitchen range on. For the next 3 days, the whole family worried that their house was probably in ashes and the goldfish were probably broiled. Their trip was ruined because they hadn't checked an important last-minute detail.

An Ohio duck hunter I know spent 6 months getting permission to hunt a swamp in Arkansas from a nonresident owner who lived in North Carolina. The owner sent the hunter a key to the big steel gate that kept the swamp private. The hunter drove all the way to Arkansas. It wasn't until he was standing before the big gate that he discovered he'd left the key in his business suit at home in Ohio.

Far in advance of a swamp-camping trip, make a list of the equipment you plan to take. To that list, add all the last-minute items and chores you must remember. As you prepare to leave, check each item as it is packed or accomplished.

Important: *After* the trip, review the list and see what was unnecessary or what was left off.

Good outfitters and guides make the use of lists a regular practice. It keeps you from forgetting to take what you need and assures you of leaving with freedom from worry. By reviewing your list when you return, you're on your way to planning better for your next trip.

LET SOMEONE KNOW

The last thing you do before you shove off into a swamp could be the most important part of your entire preparation: let a responsible person know exactly where you are going and when you plan to return. If you have a map with your route of travel marked on it, make a copy (at least a rough sketch in pencil) and leave it with that person. Emergencies do happen, both at home and in the swamp. Don't allow yourself to get into a spot where you can't be found. A sunken boat, broken leg, heart attack, lost camper, or some other emergency may make it necessary for officials to locate you. By letting someone know your plans, any needed rescue may be much quicker. If nobody knows where you are and when you plan to return, it could be days before the search begins. By then you could be dead.

12

Swamp Hunting

Though it is not the purpose of this book to teach the many interesting techniques that are used in swamp hunting (that would be a large book in itself), I would like to show several examples of how swamp hunting can be productive. Erwin Bauer, noted outdoor writer, photographer, and sportsman, once stated that swamps are possibly the richest wildlife communities on this continent. For this reason, more and more hunters are learning swamp-hunting techniques.

Here are three examples of swamp-hunting techniques that I hope will lead you to exploring on your own the many other successful techniques.

WHITETAIL DEER

Deer-hunting techniques in swamps vary throughout North America. In the Deep South, deer are run by packs of dogs. In the Far North, deer are tracked by hunters in snow at a speed that would kill most of us. There is one technique, though, that works well in

Bowhunter sits in a swamp tree overlooking an area that he believes will be visited by a whitetail buck. Fresh scrapes are a good tip-off. Credit: Florida Department of Commerce.

swamps everywhere if the season is open during the rut. This technique is known as scrape hunting.

In order to be a good scrape hunter, you must know something about the rut. Each year, sometime during the fall, bucks 1½ years old and older begin to get the urge to mate. The sexual maturity of does may start much younger. Many of them come into estrus the first time when they are from 7 to 9 months old. The estrus period of does will last for approximately 24 hours. If a doe fails to conceive during that period, she will have another period some 28 days later. If the doe still fails to conceive, this process usually repeats itself three times during the rutting season. It is not unusual for a buck to follow a doe 2 days before the estrus period and up to 2 days after.

The first sign that deer hunters will find to indicate that the rut is about to begin will be new rubs: small saplings with the bark freshly scraped off 2 to 3 feet above the ground. These rubs are made when a buck rubs his antlers on small saplings and trees in his territory. Some biologist think that the buck leaves on each of these rubs a scent from a gland near his eye.

The second sign you will find is the one that indicates the rut is happening. When a buck is in the peak of his rut, he stakes out his territory by arbitrarily making scrapes. To find a scrape, look for a pawed-out area on the ground. A scrape may vary from the size of this book to the size of a truck tire. The buck makes these scrapes by using his front foot to pull out all the leaves, grass and such from a spot of ground.

Also you'll see a bush or limb hanging down over the pawed-out area. The buck stirs up the scraped-out area with his foot and antlers. Next he will urinate in the fresh dirt and reach up and chew on the overhanging bushes.

Every few hours the buck will check his scrape to see if an interested doe has been by or if another buck has entered his territory. The visiting deer, buck or doe, that finds a scrape will usually urinate and paw in it to announce his or her presence.

Scrapes don't appear in any particular pattern or number. Sometimes you may find three or four in a row close to one another, and at other times you may find only one.

The one thing that's consistent is the type of area in which a buck likes to make scrapes. The rutting buck likes an open area such as the edge of an old field, the edge of a clearcut, an old logging road, or a thinly wooded ridgetop. If the swamp has a lot of old, unused logging roads, they will more than likely be his preference.

Scrapes are most often made by dominant bucks that are 2½ years old or older. The buck will check his scrape and freshen it at least every 2 to 3 days and maybe as often as several times in 1 day.

The hunter who is new to a swamp area will be wise to hunt scrapes. Fresh scrapes indicate that a buck is working them. Wildlife biologists tell us that bucks feed very little during the rut. In fact, they lose weight during this trying period. Rather than eat, they spend a lot of time moving about their territory. They travel at all hours and are just as likely to check their scrapes at noon as at daylight. As rutting bucks travel, they sometimes make a sound similar to the grunting of a hog.

Here are some basic guidelines for scrape hunting.

1. Learn from experienced hunters or wildlife biologists when the peak of the rut usually occurs in the area you plan to hunt.

By paying attention to scrapes, this swamp hunter knew where to be with his muzzleloader in order to take this heavy-antlered buck. Credit: Charley Dickey.

2. Thoroughly scout out your hunting area and look for scrapes along field edges, old logging roads, and ridgetops.

3. Make sure the scrapes are fresh. Ask yourself these questions: Has the dirt been disturbed lately? Does the dirt have a strong urine odor? Have the overhanging bushes been chewed? Are there fresh rubs in the area?

4. As you study the scrape area, leave as little man scent as possible. Try putting urine deer lure on your boots and trouser cuffs to cover man scent.

5. When you find fresh scrapes, squirt a few drops of urine deer lure in the scrape. Take a well-hidden stand

downwind, where you can observe the scrape and surrounding area.

6. Arrive before daylight, and stay until dark. Remain observant throughout the day and listen for any unusual sounds. Remember: the rutting buck may make sounds like the grunting of a hog.

7. In hilly areas, concentrate on scrapes that are on or near the tops of ridges or in creek bottoms and have bedding areas nearby.

8. Plan to spend at least 3 days watching the scrapes. As with most types of hunting, patience and constant alertness are most important for successful scrape hunting.

SQUIRRELS

Since before Daniel Boone's time, squirrel hunting has been a top sport in the United States. Several years ago, I tried a different method of squirrel hunting along a river swamp, and I found it quite an adventure. An old friend in Georgia called me and asked if I wanted to combine a canoe trip and squirrel hunt down a section of a swamp river near his home. Being interested in both canoeing and squirrel hunting, I readily accepted the invitation.

A week later, daybreak found us paddling our way down the misty river. During the first few minutes, we could see very little. But we could already hear squirrels barking. As the silent canoe slid through the water, yellow and pink fingers of light stretched across the sky and changed into a rising sun that soon melted the mist.

Then the action started! It seemed that almost every tree along the slow-moving river had a silvertail jumping in it.

By late afternoon we were camping on a beautiful sandbar with two limits of squirrels and with thoughts of maybe fishing tomorrow. It had been a complete day.

Successfully canoeing for squirrels, like any other hunt, requires proper planning and equipment. And as in any outdoor adventure, the planning is a lot of fun.

If you don't own a canoe, locate either a friend with a canoe you can borrow, a rent-all store that has canoes, or a canoe outfitter. Try to get a 14- to 17-foot canoe, especially if you plan to camp. Canoes of such size are likely to be fairly stable and also able to carry plenty of weight.

After locating a canoe, learn basic canoeing skills and canoeing safety. Practice these skills with the canoe in the water until you feel comfortable in the craft. At this point you should get your hunting pardner involved in learning how to canoe safely. You both should become proficient before starting out on a hunt. Canoeing instruction is usually available through canoe shops, YMCAs, your local Red Cross office, and your local canoe club. Some community colleges also offer canoeing instruction.

When your canoeing skills are sharpened, find a stream that has suitable stream-bank habitat for squirrels. You will be looking for mature woodlands made up of beech, hickory, and oak trees. You will also want to select a stream that has bridge or road access at convenient put-in (upper) and take-out (lower) points. These two points should be from 5 to 10 miles apart for your first few trips. The distance will depend on speed of stream flow, amount of hunting time you have, difficulty of obstacles, and whether or not you plan to camp. In a few trips, you will learn how to plan the trip distance.

The put-in and take-out points are also important to the logistics of the trip. On the day of the hunt, you'll want to have someone drop you off at the upper point and pick you up at a prearranged time at the lower point. Or you can follow your hunting pardner with the canoe on your car to the lower point, leave his car, and both of you take your car to the upper point. With this method, take the canoe carrier with you in the canoe. At the end of the trip, you load the canoe onto his car and then drive to pick up your car.

I have found that one good way to locate an unknown squirrel hunting stream is to visit the county agent, conservation officer, forester, or soil conservationist in the county you wish to hunt. These officials usually know of a section of river or stream that best suits your needs. I have also found that these officials know the stream-bank landowners and can help with getting permission to hunt and camp on their land. Getting permission is most important, and you should explain to the landowner how you plan to hunt and that there will be no danger of your committing such offenses as leaving open gates or parking in the wrong place. You will come quietly and go by canoe.

Many excellent squirrel-hunting streams are found on state and federal lands, and one permit usually does the job. I have also found oak-bordered streams on public hunting areas and, after leaving the put-in point at a bridge, saw no other hunters until I neared the bridge at the lower part of the trip.

Another method of finding suitable streams is to study county road maps and U.S. Geological Survey maps. Not only are these maps helpful in locating streams but they are also useful in such trip-planning details as computing distances and locating campsites.

The more detailed maps may also show water hazards such as rapids and waterfalls. No trip should be planned for an unfamiliar stream without first talking with someone who has made the trip. Rapids, waterfalls, and other obstacles can turn an enjoyable trip into a nightmare for the unsuspecting. Good stream knowledge should be a part of the trip planning and you should get up-to-date stream conditions before the trip begins.

Your basic equipment for such a trip should include a portable canoe carrier, two canoe paddles, life preser-

Improbable though it might seem, a fisherman's dip net is an essential part of the equipment for retrieving squirrels downed during swamp hunt.

vers, one shotgun, shells, camouflage clothing, and a dip net. I have found the portable canoe carriers made from Ethafoam blocks are the easiest to handle, especially if you take them with you in the canoe. Only one shotgun is needed. It is safer and much more efficient for only the person in the front of the canoe to do the shooting. You can take turns shooting and work as a team. A 20-gauge shotgun loaded with No. 6 shot does well. A dip net is necessary as it takes little time for a floating squirrel to become soaked and sink.

Using a canoe to hunt squirrels has many advantages. The canoe itself is quiet, can be maneuvered easily, can be carried around and over obstacles without much effort, and can cover a lot of miles in a hurry if necessary.

River bottoms are usually among the most game-rich areas in any region. Many times when there are but a few squirrels in the ridges, there will be many in the river bottoms, especially during dry years.

Canoe hunting for squirrels is versatile and can include camping, fishing, or photography. It can be a morning's hunt, or it can fill a 3-day weekend. It is a great way to start a young outdoorsman in swamp camping.

DUCKS

Many of us greatly enjoy standing knee-deep in an icy swamp while the mallards set their wings and come in on the decoys. As I mentioned earlier in this book, beavers are creating new swamps every year. Many of these small swamps can, with a little work, be made into duck areas. Here is how you can have great swamp duck hunting.

In many areas, you'll discover opportunities to turn a beaver swamp into an area for duck shooting. You'll need to invest some thought and some physical work. Credit: Denise Huddleston.

First get in touch with your local forestry, game-and-fish, or soil-conservation office to locate the beaver swamps in your area. Visit these swamps, and look for one that has at least 3 acres of shallow water (2 to 30 inches deep). Most of the standing trees in the pond should be dead.

After you've located a suitable beaver swamp, work out a lease or other agreement with the landowner so that you may develop his beaver swamp into your duck pond. Of course you must observe whatever state regulations apply.

Your development should begin in mid-June by breaking the beaver dam at the existing channel. This break should be made in the form of a narrow, deep "V." Allow several hours for water to drain from the pond area. When the flow of water has slackened enough for you to work with ease, install a three-log drain.

1. Start with three main logs, two on the bottom and one on the top. These logs should be about 7 to 10 inches in diameter and 10 to 16 feet long. They should be green or waterlogged, for weight. Keep these main logs slightly separated by using spacers made of green sticks about 2 inches in diameter. Fasten the three main logs, so arranged, into a unit by using nails or wire.

2. Place a piece of roofing metal over the top log, and then bend it down, as shown, and nail it to the two bottom logs.

3. At the bottom of the break in the dam, place another piece of roofing metal, this one approximately 2½ feet wide and 6 to 8 feet long. Place the three-log drain on top of this metal base. Bend this piece of metal up on both sides, and nail it to the two bottom logs. The upstream end of the log drain should be completely covered by water and at least 1 foot *lower* than the outlet

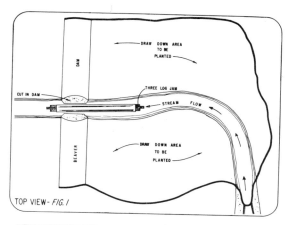

TOP VIEW- *FIG. I*

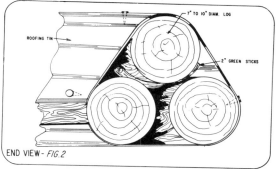

END VIEW- *FIG.2*

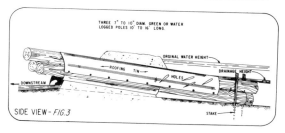

SIDE VIEW- *FIG.3*

These three views show the basic ideas described in the text that are involved in building and installing a three-log drain for a beaver pond. Some slight variations are, of course, possible. In any event, be certain you have permission of the landowner and are working in accordance with conservation agencies and state law. Credit: Adapted from a design by U.S.D.A.

(downstream) end of the log drain. The drain's outlet end should be propped up solidly; the upstream end should be firmly staked in place. Pile some mud and sticks on top of the drain. With this three-log drain in place, the beaver pond will be reduced to a channel of water. Usually the beavers cannot figure out why their dam leaks, but occasionally they manage to stop it. Until you are ready to flood the pond later in the year, the three-log drain should be checked weekly to keep it open and free-flowing.

After you've successfully drawn down the water, the next step is to sow the exposed mud flats with Japanese-millet seed at the rate of 20 pounds per acre. It is important that only Japanese-millet seed be used, as other plants will not grow satisfactorily under beaver-pond conditions. The sowing can best be done by using a cyclone seeder and wading through the mud. Japanese-millet seed requires moist ground, and the best conditions seem to be ankle-deep mud. No further land preparation is needed. Fertilizer is usually not necessary the first 2 years. The Japanese millet will mature in approximately 60 days, so plant it in time to mature before the first frost.

By the time the millet has matured, you should have your duck blinds constructed and be ready to flood the planted area.

Flooding your duck pond is done by removing the three-log drain and letting the beavers plug the hole. If the beavers are slow in doing the job, a few sandbags will work just about as well.

Since most beaver swamps converted into duck ponds are small, shooting management is a must. You cannot shoot ducks on these small ponds from dawn until dark and expect the ducks to stay. For best results, start by shooting ducks on your pond only one morning each

Among the species of game animals and gamebirds found in the swamp, the wild turkey is high on the spring and fall lists of many hunters.

week. Then let experience determine how often you can shoot.

The same pond-management procedure is necessary each year—with a few changes. Occasionally, the original seeding of millet provides enough hard seed so that further seeding is not necessary. But don't depend on it. The most reliable approach is to reseed each year. Though fertilizer usually isn't necessary until the third year, check with your county agent if the millet plants in your duck pond are slow to grow. They may need fertilizer.

The only physical prerequisites for a duck pond are beavers to build dams and a climate that has at least approximately 60 frost-free days necessary for Japanese millet to grow a mature seed crop. Most of the United States has that many days without frost.

As with any venture, experience will help you make your duck pond more productive each year. It's hard to find a better solution to your problem of where to hunt ducks.

Wild turkey in spring or fall, raccoons, wild hogs, and many other species of game animals can be hunted in the swamp. And with a little experience, you'll find that the winter swamp camp can be one of the best hunting camps you will ever enjoy.

13

Swamp Fishing

Swamp fishing varies in many ways from lake fishing. In lakes we fish structure, but in swamps we fish cover. Because of the shallow water and the vast number of trees, logs, weeds, lilies, and so on in swamps, cover is found everywhere. So fish are like to be caught just about everywhere in swamps.

A veteran lake fisherman, in order to fish swamps, must learn the importance of casting accuracy. Under most swamp conditions, flyrods are tough to use and spinning or bait-casting tackle is recommended.

The casts are usually around trees, beside trees, between trees, over logs and in similar tight places. Seldom are the casts long unless you fish the open water commonly called swamp holes. These deeper holes, properly fished, can produce lunkers, but more about that in a moment.

Lures used in swamp fishing are most often weedless spoons, spinner baits, and unweighted worms. In swamp holes or more open waters, topwater plugs and small spinners are common.

For fishing this swamp hole and most other swamp areas, the recommended equipment is either bait-casting or spinning tackle. Credit: Georgia Industry & Trade.

As with all other types of fishing, swamp-fishing techniques, baits, lures, and species of fish vary from one part of the country to the other. Here are a few samples of fishing techniques that produce lunkers in most swamps.

LARGEMOUTH BASS

Spring is the prime fishing period for the largemouth. On warm days during February, March, and April, the bass move into shallow water to begin "bedding." It is during this time that many lunker largemouth are caught by anglers using an assortment of plastic worms and No. 4 weedless hooks. During summer and fall, fishing early in the morning and late in the afternoon with topwater plugs—particularly Rapala, Rebel, and Devils Horse—can produce a healthy string of lunkers. Cast these topwater plugs in open water, to the edge of lilies, or at the base of trees.

A method that swampers use during the hot months is to float around water lilies late in the afternoon and look for small patches of open water (swamp holes). Paddle with little disturbance to within range and cast into the opening a black plastic worm with a No. 4 weedless hook stuck through its center. Let the worm settle to the bottom. By then you should feel a slight tugging. If so, count to ten, set the hook, and hold on. This method has produced many a lunker largemouth in swamps. It is best to use a 15- to 20-pound test line. Most of the "ponds" are weedy and contain many obstacles that favor the hooked largemouth.

If open patches of water are difficult to find, try casting a black weedless spoon or black weed wing with pork rind into the weeds or lily pads, and bring it back across slowly. Often this tactic will cause an explosion as a large bass goes after the intruder. A stiff-action rod and heavy line are musts for this fishing.

In thick vegetation such as that in cypress swamps, unweighted worms cast beside such objects as logs, trees, and weeds are often deadly on largemouth.

BLUEGILL

Many swamps produce lunker bluegills in the 1-pound category, particularly during the bedding period (from early May through August). During this period, native swamp fishermen "smell out" bream beds. Early in the morning, they drift around the stumps and lilies in the swamps, their noses high in the air. When they locate a fishy-smelling area, they break out the cane poles and bait up with worms or crickets. Stump by stump and lily pad by lily pad, they drop their bait nearby until the bed is found. Then they catch a mess of bluegills.

I know several swamp fishermen who have worked out a method of catching lunker bluegills (in the 2-pound class) during the hot summer and fall periods. These experts fish the deeper parts of the swamps, which are usually free of obstacles, with an ultralight spinning outfit rigged with "The Thing" or with a spinner followed by a Shuman Cricket. They say this fishing is as much fun as landing a 12-pound largemouth bass on heavy tackle, and it does catch lunker bluegills when most fishermen are sitting it out in the shade.

One method of fishing for bluegills along swamp rivers is called pitching. Take a short, slender cane pole (usually 6 to 8 feet long) and tie to its tip a length of 6-

A string that includes bluegills and other panfish means the addition of some tasty protein to the menu of these swamp campers.

pound-test monofilament line the same length as the pole. Use a No. 10 or No. 8 hook.

With this short rig and several dozen crickets, savvy fishermen silently float the river. The idea is to toss a cricket next to logs, stumps, and cypress knees. When the bluegill or sunfish hits, you get a sporty fight on the short rig.

NORTHERN PIKE

This northern swamp fish is usually found around water lilies or weed beds. The pike will usually fall for a weedless spoon with a pork frog or for a weedless hook with a jumbo frog. Use a wire leader to keep the pike's teeth from cutting your line. Cast to the middle of the green vegetation, and retrieve the lure slowly. Make it crawl off one lily pad and onto another. Your quarry will usually hit when the lure drops into open water.

CHAIN PICKEREL

Commonly called "jack" by swampers, this fighting fish is found in many swamps and may be caught at any time the law allows. The world record, a 9-pound 6-ounce lunker, was caught in a swamp near Homerville, Georgia. The best way to catch jacks is to locate swamp holes and to cast to the center of the open water with Mepps spinners or Yellow Shyster. If the jacks are rolling, you're in luck. Just cast to each roll and hold on to your rod.

CRAPPIE

The crappie, though not usually thought of as a swamp fish, is a popular fish in many swamps that have areas of open, deeper water.

It is fun to fish for crappies at night. Excellent fishing can be produced by hanging a gas lantern over the side of a boat. Special holders for lanterns are available at most leading sporting-goods outlets. Fishing experts will tell you that the lantern attracts bugs and insects, many of which will fall to the water below the lantern. Forage fish and minnows feed on the bugs, and the crappies prowl after the forage fish and minnows.

If you're fortunate enough on a warm spring or summer night to be in such a spot with light tackle and a few minnows, jigs, spinners, or other baits, it's a pretty good bet that you can catch fish. Thousands of crappies, white bass, perch, and bluegills are caught this way each year. Once in a while, northern pike and largemouth bass also are taken this way.

In many areas, fishing by day in the summertime is a hot proposition. But a light breeze in a swamp at night usually brings a break in the heat. Nights in a swamp can be a time for you and your fishing friends to find enjoyment, relaxation, and true peace in the great outdoors.

One of the most fascinating parts of swamp fishing is that you never know what you may catch. Stringers often include the fish I've already mentioned, but you may also catch bowfin, gar, carp, sunfish, and catfish. With this wide variety of fish available, a swamp camper has no reason to leave his frying pan at home.

If you are tired of large reservoirs, bass-boat hot-rodders, and water skiers, take to the swamp. The fishing is about as simple as it was in the good old days. You won't be bothered by a lot of noise and waves. But you might have to share a good fishing hole with another fisherman such as an otter or a water turkey (anhinga).

14

Other Swamp Adventures

The swamp camper has a choice of many adventures. He is limited only by his imagination, experience, and interest.

WILDLIFE STUDY AND PHOTOGRAPHY

Swamps are rich in wildlife. There is, perhaps, no better place in the country to find such a variety of wildlife and view it at close range. I advise any swamp camper to take along a pair of binoculars and guidebooks to birds, reptiles, amphibians, or whatever may be your interest.

It's amazing how fast you can become an amateur naturalist by spending a little time studying the inhabitants of the swamp. As you become familiar with the swamp critters, you'll find that your camping, hunting, and fishing skills will also improve. The better we understand our environment, the better we can live in it.

If you're an amateur photographer, the swamp gives you a chance to bring home trophies on film even when the hunting season is closed.

The swamp environment provides unmatched opportunities to see wildlife such as these roseate spoonbills at close range. Credit: National Park Service.

If, to the study of wildlife, you add the sport of photography, you'll find yourself a year-round hunter. Taking trophies on film is a very satisfying skill in itself. In very few other places will critters pose for you the way they do in the swamp.

BOWFISHING

Many states permit bowfishing for so-called trash fish. These species are generally carp and gar. Many swamps in the backwaters of lakes, river-bottom swamps, and swamps in general have a good population of these fish.

The sport of bowfishing is very exciting. Once you try it, it's hard not to go again. The equipment consists of a bow, fishing-line reel (bow reel), which is attached to the bow, and a fish arrow with line running from it to the reel.

By riding in the prow of a wide, stable, slow-moving boat while wearing Polaroid sunglasses, you can see down into the water. When a target presents itself, you shoot. If you're on target, you have a fight on your hands.

Many bowfishermen, including myself, prefer to wade while they bowfish. This approach is especially effective when hunting carp. It is not unusual for a bowfisherman to have a 20-pound carp or a 50-pound gar on the end of his line. When this happens, you're hooked. You'll become an avid bowfisherman.

FROG GIGGING

An enjoyable sideline during summer swamp-camping trips is to take a night off to go frog gigging. Around most swamps, many bullfrogs are available to anybody who's not squeamish about pushing a boat under overhanging limbs or through thick bushes. At

A swamp is likely to have a good population of rough fish such as this carp. Many states allow you to shoot rough fish with bow and arrow. **Credit: Georgia Industry & Trade.**

night, the big frogs sit on land next to the water and sing out in their base tones.

Two people get into a boat or canoe. One paddles, and the other wears a head-mounted electric light and holds the long handle of a five-prong frog gig. As you ease along the edge of islands and other high areas in the swamp, you shine the light and hope to spot a bullfrog. This is one sport in which you can almost be assured of seeing snakes at close range. The rewards, however, are well worth the problems. Few meals equal golden-fried frog legs. If you decide to take up this exciting sport, try this recipe that I got from John Phillips, master outdoorsman and frog gigger of Fairfield, Alabama.

Frogs' Legs Sauté—3 pounds frogs' legs (12-18 large pairs), flour (optional), ¼ cup of butter, 1 teaspoon of salt, ¼ teaspoon of pepper, juice of ½ lemon, and 2 tablespoons of minced parsley (garnish). If the frogs' legs are tiny, count on eight pairs per person. If really large, three pairs. Wash and pat dry. Dust with flour, if you wish. Sauté in butter until brown, turn and brown other side. Sprinkle with salt, pepper, and lemon juice. Put on hot platter, pour the butter over them, and sprinkle with parsley. Makes four to six servings.

Once you try a batch of sautéed frog legs, you'll find yourself at every opportunity under snakey-looking bushes at night in a swamp.

15

Directory of Some Important Swamps

Throughout our country are countless swamps of various sizes. To list them all would require several books. The following brief introduction to our major swamps will give you a start in deciding which swamps you want to see. Each swamp listed has a source from which you can get more information.

Everglades National Park—In southern Florida, just west of Miami, lies one of our largest swamps—the Everglades. Its 13,000 square miles are made up of mangrove-covered islands, channels, sawgrass prairies, pine upland, and cypress-studded ponds. Hunting is prohibited, but fishing is allowed in most areas of the park.

The park has several campgrounds with complete facilities. You may also camp at designated sites on the

In southern Florida, just west of Miami, is Everglades National Park. Hunting is prohibited, but fishing is allowed in most areas of the park. Credit: National Park Service.

beaches or in the backcountry, where access is by boat or on foot only. You must first get a backcountry-use permit from park officials.

For more information, write: Everglades National Park, Box 279, Homestead, Florida 33030.

Big Cypress Swamp—This 2,450-square-mile swamp is one of the less-developed swamps in the country. It is rich in wildlife and one of the last swamps in which the endangered Florida panther is found. The swamp has some largemouth-bass fishing. But severe water-table fluctuation makes fishing somewhat limited. Some 570,000 acres of the swamp were designated as a national water preserve in 1974. However, the swamp does permit hunting. The Big Cypress is on the northern boundary of the Everglades National Park.

For more information write: Florida Game & Fresh Water Fish Commission, 620 S. Meridian Street, Tallahassee, Florida 32304.

Florida's Swamp Rivers—Florida has many swamp rivers, which abound in game, fish, and scenic beauty. Five of these rivers have outfitters who can take you on a variety of paddling adventures. These rivers are Peace, Suwannee, Withlacoochee, Alafia, and St. Mary's. Together they offer over 500 miles of river for you to see.

For more information write: Canoe Outpost, Rt. 2, Box 301, Arcadia, Florida 33821.

Okefenokee Swamp—Okefenokee Swamp, a 681-square-mile peat-filled bog in Georgia's Ware, Charlton, and Clinch counties and Florida's Baker county, is one of the nation's great unspoiled areas. Although a considerable amount of timber has been harvested here in past years, most of this great swamp has changed little from what it was when first seen by white men. About ⅘ of the swamp is included in the Okefenokee National Wildlife Refuge, which is administered by the Bureau of Sport Fisheries and Wildlife, U.S. Fish and Wildlife Service, in the Department of the Interior.

Except for some fifty islands that total about 25,000

In some parts of the Okefenokee Swamp, hunting is permitted. The swamp's fishing is excellent. Credit: Georgia Industry & Trade.

acres, Okefenokee Swamp is usually shallowly flooded. Most of the flooded area is more or less densely forested with cypress, blackgum, bay, and maple—with an understory and interspersal of various heaths, similax, titi, and cassena. About 60,000 acres is flooded marshland or "prairie," which is covered principally with waterlilies, neverwet, pipewort, ferns, maidencane, and a variety of sedges and grasses.

Though hunting is not permitted in the wildlife refuge, it is allowed on other parts of the swamp and surrounding area. Fishing in the swamp is excellent.

Around the swamp are several campgrounds, including two state parks. Camping in the swamp is permitted by special permission only, and it is restricted to platforms along the canoe trails. Travel is permissible only on designated trails. The swamp has two interesting interpretive centers—one at the Okefenokee Swamp Park near Waycross, Georgia, and one at the Suwannee Canal Recreation Area near Folkston, Georgia. Guides are available for trips into the heart of the swamp.

For more information write: Okefenokee National Wildlife Refuge, P. O. Box 117, Waycross, Georgia 31501.

Alapaha and Withlacoochee Rivers—Two of Georgia's many swamp rivers are the Alapaha and the Withlacoochee. These rivers flow through some of the most remote areas of south Georgia. The hunting and fishing along the rivers is good, and a float down either river is well worth the trip.

For more information write: Coastal Plain APDC, P. O. Box 1223, Valdosta, Georgia 31601.

The Great Swamp of Rhode Island—One of New England's best-known swamps is the Great Swamp of Rhode Island. This glacier-formed swamp is the home of many species of wildlife and is managed by the Rhode Island Department of Natural Resources as a wildlife-management area. Each year deer hunts are held in the swamp.

For more information write: Department of Natural Resources, Division of Fish and Wildlife, 83 Park Street, Providence, Rhode Island 02903.

Mingo Swamp—Located in southeastern Missouri, the Mingo Swamp is a typical river-bottom swamp made by the changing course of the Mississippi River. Over 21,000 acres of the swamp is managed by the U.S. Fish and Wildlife Service as the Mingo National Wildlife Refuge. A tract of 1,700 acres in the swamp has been set aside as the Black Mingo Wilderness Area and travel there is only by foot or canoe. Fishermen find the swamp productive for largemouth bass, bluegills, and crappies. Hunters find deer and squirrels abundant.

For more information write: Mingo National Wildlife Refuge, Rt. 1, Box 9A, Puxico, Missouri 63960.

Reelfoot Lake—Reelfoot Lake and its surrounding swamps in western Tennessee were formed by a series of violent earth tremors in late 1811 and early 1812.

More than 15,000 acres of forest land sank, and the resulting hole was filled with water from the nearby Mississippi River. The lake and swamp are now known as Reelfoot Lake. Reelfoot is probably one of the best hunting, fishing, and camping swamps in the nation. The U.S. Fish and Wildlife Service has set aside the upper reaches of Reelfoot as a National Wildlife Refuge, while the state of Tennessee has set up another portion as the Reelfoot Wildlife Management Area. Each year hunts are held for doves, wild turkey, rabbit, whitetail deer, squirrels, and ducks. Fishing in the lake and swamp is well known, and stringers of striped bass, largemouth bass, bluegill, crappie, and carp make the area most appealing. Ged Petit of the Tennessee Wildlife Resources Agency gave this report on fishing at Reelfoot.

"Our sample rotenone studies reveal that the 10,000-acre lake holds about 1,200 pounds of fish to the acre—

we have nothing else in the state that comes anywhere near equaling this poundage. Our creel studies, which have been in progress since the 1950s, reveal that anglers catch more fish per hour of effort in Reelfoot than in any other lake we have. I doubt that any other lake in the United States has a better catch rate. I've never seen one documented. The success rate on the lake runs from 85 to 90 percent on an annual basis. That means when our creel clerk checks anglers, 9 out of 10 have taken at least one fish. A fisheries biologist considers this success rate extremely high. Most of our lakes have from 30 to 55 percent success rate."

Camping at Reelfoot is available at Reelfoot State Park, private campgrounds, and in the backcountry. Like many of our larger swamps, parts of Reelfoot are inaccessible except by canoe, and a guide is recommended.

For more information write: Wildlife Communications Coordinator, Tennessee Wildlife Resources Agency, 1184 Highway 45 Bypass, Jackson, Tennessee 38301.

The Great Dismal Swamp—This 750-square-mile swamp is on the eastern part of the boundary between Virginia and North Carolina. The heart of this vast swamp is Lake Drummond, a circular lake that covers nearly 3,000 acres. Its average depth is only 6 feet, but the unusually pure water, preserved by the barks of the juniper, gum, and cypress trees, is essential to the swamp's survival. Some 70 square miles of the swamp is in the Dismal Swamp National Wildlife Refuge, and 22 square miles is in the Dismal Swamp State Park. A large portion of the swamp is owned by timber companies and paper companies. Some 20,000 acres of their land is managed by the state of North Carolina for public hunting in the Dismal Swamp Game Land. Fishing is found throughout the swamp. Lake Drummond is within the National Wildlife Refuge, and access is permitted from sunrise to sunset. Camping is available at the Corps of Engineers' Lake Drummond Reservation, at the Dismal State Park, and in the swamp, except the part in the National Wildlife Refuge.

For more information write: Dismal Swamp State Park, Rt. 1, Box 41, Corapeake, North Carolina 27926. North Carolina Wildlife Resources Commission, Division of Game, 325 N. Salisbury Street, Raleigh, North Carolina 27611. Dismal Swamp National Wildlife Refuge, P. O. Box 349, Suffolk, Virginia 23434.

The Big Thicket of Texas—Some 75 miles northeast of Houston, Texas, is a large area in which the ecology of the Southwest meets and mingles with that of the Southeast. The swamp, encompassing some 300,000 acres, is called the Big Thicket. It is rich in game, fish, wilderness, and legend. One eastern writer described it as a treacherous place. "It is dotted with pools of oozing slime," he said, "and guarded by swarms of angry black bears, by alligators, ferocious wild pigs, and all four species of poisonous snakes found in this country, not to mention a nude hermit who, legend has it, carries a loaded pistol in each hand."

Much of the Big Thicket is privately owned, but some 84,000 acres has been set aside as the Big Thicket National Preserve. The preserve has hunting, fishing, and camping opportunities that could keep a swamp camper active for years. Contrary to the eastern writer's description of the Big Thicket, it is a sportsman's paradise.

In the Big Thicket of Texas, the ecology of the Southwest meets and mingles with the ecology of the Southeast. The area is rich in animals, fish, wilderness, and legend. Credit: National Park Service.

For more information write: Big Thicket National Preserve, P. O. Box 7408, Beaumont, Texas 77706.

South Carolina River Swamps—Perhaps some of the best river swamps left in North America are found in South Carolina. Here are examples of four of the rivers.

Wateree River This slow-moving, meandering river offers a float through undisturbed wilderness and managed forest lands. The Wateree's eastern bank is almost entirely swampland. Deer, turkey, wild hog, alligator, and all types of birdlife abound in the vast river swamp.

Camping is available along the river at bars and high banks, but floaters who camp on sandbars or gravel bars should be aware of the river's daily fluctuation according to the need for electrical power at the Lake Wateree Dam above the town of Camden.

Black River Best known for its bleached sandbars and fiery redbreast sunfish, the Black River is perhaps the state's most pristine low-country stream. The river's path takes it almost entirely through undisturbed wild lands.

Camping is available on many unspoiled sandbars and river bluffs. Floaters who take to the river in late summer, however, should be aware that the river's upper portions may be very shallow from lack of rain. Wildlife species such as deer, alligator, otter, and all bird types are common.

Little Pee Dee River Swamps, dead lakes (oxbows), and many feeder creeks characterize this blackwater stream.

Wildlife, including alligator, beaver, otter, deer, turkey, wild hogs, and all bird types, are plentiful.

Camping is available along the river's many sandbars and bluffs. Floaters who wish to take only a 1-day trip may readily do so by using one of the public landings.

Edisto River One of South Carolina's most scenic blackwater rivers, the Edisto, offers floaters the chance to view a wide variety of wildlife. Alligators, bobcats, otters, turkey, whitetail deer, and almost uncountable species of birds are among the river swamp's denizens.

Though the river's surface seems calm, swimmers should beware of the current's underwater force. Many submerged snags and trees also add to this hazard for the uncautious.

Camping is available along the river's many sandbars and high banks on the northernmost stretches of the river. Public and private campgrounds are available below Highway 15.

Fishing and hunting in these river swamps is excellent.

For more information write: Wildlife and Marine Resources Department, Box 167, Columbia, South Carolina 29202.

Mobile River Delta—Down in the extreme lower southwestern corner of Alabama lies the Mobile River Delta. The delta begins at the confluence of the Tombigbee and Alabama Rivers and continues some 40 miles to the marshes of Mobile Bay. This large delta contains hundreds of bass-filled oxbows and sloughs. The setting is one of the most beautiful swamps to be found anywhere, and wildlife abounds. The Mobile River

Delta is bounded on the west by U.S. Highway 43 and on the east by Alabama Highways 7 and 59. Some 40 boat-landing and fishing camps are scattered throughout the delta. Largemouth bass and bull blue-gills are the major species of this area. Crappies, sunfish, and catfish are also available. The vastness and beauty of this area, coupled with the uncrowded fishing, make it one of the best fishing areas in the country.

Hunting in the area is excellent for whitetail deer and wild turkey. Camping opportunities are almost limitless, especially if you travel by canoe.

For more information write: Alabama Division of Game and Fish, 64 North Union Street, Montgomery, Alabama 36104. Canoe Trails, Rt. 7, Box 429, Mobile, Alabama 36608.

Honey Island Swamp—Along the Louisiana-Mississippi line, where the Pearl River flows to the Gulf of Mexico, lies one of our nation's least explored swamps—Honey Island. The swamp encompasses an estimated 250 square miles of river delta and is rich in folklore, fishing, hunting, and camping. Some 15,000 acres of the swamp is managed by the Louisiana Wildlife and Fisheries Commission as a wildlife sanctuary. The remaining land is owned by several large companies, and most of it is open to the public. Besides its hunting and fishing and being a great place to explore, the swamp is best known for the creature that is supposed to roam its depths. The creature has added much to a swamp that was already overrun with legends. If you want to explore, Honey Island Swamp is a great place to start.

For more information write: Louisiana Wildlife and Fisheries Commission, 400 Royal Street, New Orleans,

Louisiana 70130. Byron Almquist, Canoe and Trail Shop, 624 Moss Street, New Orleans, Louisiana 70119.

Pascagoula River Swamp—Flowing down through southeast Mississippi is the Pascagoula River. It and the land in its flood plain and tributaries make up an interesting swamp complex. Recently the state of Mississippi bought 32,000 acres along the river for a game-management area. The Black Creek flows into the Pascagoula and is considered one of the most scenic float streams anywhere. The Black's normal flow rate is about 1 mile per hour, making it a perfect trip for canoes or johnboats. The water is clear, and the banks are lined with cypress trees. As in most small streams, the fish (bass and bluegill) aren't big, but they are good fighters. There are many oxbow lakes along the Pascagoula River, and some are connected to the river. Others may be found on maps. By using some swamp navigation, you can reach them on foot. The fishing is worth the trip. Hunting in the area is good for deer, wild turkey, and small game.

For more information write: Mississippi Game and Fish Commission, P.O. Box 451, Jackson, Mississippi 39205.

Atchafalaya Swamp—One of the largest swamps found in North America, the Atchafalaya Swamp is in the heart of the Louisiana Bayou country. This vast swamp, approximately 1,300 square miles, is formed by water flowing out of the Mississippi River, down the Atchafalaya River into the Gulf of Mexico. The most frequent visitors to the swamp are fishermen. These waters are widely known for largemouth bass, bluegills, crappies, and catfish. Hunters are also discovering the rewards of the Atchafalaya. Deer, waterfowl, and small game are taken in the swamp. Like many of our great swamps, the Atchafalaya is in danger of being ruined by development. It is rich in oil and gas. The swamp is also receiving silt from the Mississippi River. Because of the shallow water, travel in the swamp is somewhat limited to canoe. Although the Atchafalaya Swamp has problems, it is still a vast swamp that's worth any sportsman's visit.

For more information write: Louisiana Wildlife and Fisheries Commission, 400 Royal Street, New Orleans, Louisiana 70130. Byron Almquist, Canoe and Trail Shop, 624 Moss Street, New Orleans, Louisiana 70119.

Alakai Swamp—One of the most unusual swamps in the United States is Hawaii's Alakai on the island of Kauai. This 27-square-mile swamp is 4,000 feet above sea level, which puts it out of reach of mosquitoes. The swamp is largely unexplored even though much of it is not covered by water. The Alakai has a high rainfall, up to 200 inches per year, and it has been known to rain 30 inches in 1 day. These factors have kept many would-be explorers out of the swamp. Also tending to discourage adventurers are the swamp's inaccessibility (it has cliffs on three sides) and the sudden dense fogs. There is a hunting season in this strange swamp for wild pigs, but very few hunters make the hunt. The lush vegetation makes it is easy to get lost in Alakai, and some sportsmen who went into the swamp have never returned.

For more information write: Department of Land and Natural Resources, Division of Fish and Game, 1151 Punchbowl Street, Honolulu, Hawaii 96813.

LaRue Swamp—One of our more northern flood-plain swamps is the LaRue Swamp in southern Illinois along the Big Muddy River. The swamp is part of the LaRue-Pine Hills Ecological Area of the Shawnee National Forest. This swamp is somewhat of an example of the many flood-plain swamps along the Mississippi River from Minnesota to Mississippi. The LaRue is rich in fish, waterfowl, and small game. The swamp also serves as a living laboratory for ecological studies. Travel in the LaRue and similar swamps is best accomplished by canoe.

For more information write: Public Information Officer, U.S.D.A. Forest Service, 633 W. Wisconsin Avenue, Milwaukee, Wisconsin 53203.

Great Cypress Swamp of Delaware—An excellent example of how some swamps are being saved by man is the Great Cypress Swamp of Delaware. A group called the Delaware Wild Lands, Inc. saw the Great Cypress Swamp disappearing. They raised money through donations and began buying back the swamp and restoring it to its original wild condition. Today the Great Cypress Swamp has 10,000 acres under protection.

If swamps are to remain a part of our outdoor heritage, more groups need to adopt a swamp as did these farsighted citizens of Delaware.

For more information write: Delaware Wildlands, Inc., 5806 Kennett Pike, Wilmington, Delaware 19807.

These swamps I've listed are just a small sample of what is sitting out there waiting for you to discover them. As the beaver regains parts of his territory in many parts of the country, he is creating small swamps. Swamps are all around most of us. As I stated at the beginning of this book, there are swamps in almost every state. Don't be limited to the swamps I have described. You can now begin to explore and add your newfound swamps to the list. Maybe someday we can all pool our swamp information and do a directory of swamps. On the other hand, we may want to keep them hidden away from the heavy hand of progress.

16

Three Swamp-Camping Trips for Beginners

I know of three swamp-camping trips that are particularly suitable for the less-experienced swamp camper. For this reason, I'll describe each of these trips in some detail.

THE ALAPAHA RIVER CANOE TRAIL

In Georgia just a few miles east of Interstate 75, one of the busiest highways in the nation, lies one of the South's most beautiful swamp rivers—the Alapaha. For generations, the Alapaha River has been known only to local fishermen. Beginning as a small creek near the town of Ocilla, the Alapaha grows as it flows southward to its destination, a sinkhole near the Georgia-Florida line. There it disappears underground.

It is the lower 83 miles of the river that the Coastal Plain Tourism Council, headquartered in Valdosta, has established as a river trail designed primarily for canoes. Almost as if planned, the 83-mile river trail is divided into five 1-day trips by the highways that cross it (the only development to be seen on the trail). The trail begins near the community of Willacoochee, where Georgia 135 crosses the river, and ends 83 miles later where U.S. 94 crosses near the community of Statenville.

Canoeists who want to float the entire length of the trail can easily make the trip in 5 days, with four overnight camps along the way. The tourism council has set up four primitive campsites along the trail. The use of these campsites as well as the river trail is free.

The river is ideal for family canoe camping. As it flows through the heart of south Georgia's swamp and timberland, the slow-moving river crooks and turns between high sand banks. Many of the turns produce snow-white sandbars, especially during periods of low water. Rapids are found along the river, particularly during periods of low water. The experienced canoeist can easily run them, and the inexperienced canoeist can easily pull a canoe around them. The Alapaha has been classified by canoeists as a Class 1 river, meaning easy to float.

It's a beautiful river with its forest border or tupelo, live oak, pine, and moss-covered cypress sprinkled with ever-blooming wildflowers. Since the river is fairly narrow, many times the trees reach out to form a roof over the canoeist.

Traveling in a quiet canoe, you can see much of the wildlife that lives within the river corridor. Beaver, otter, wood duck, wild turkey, and deer are almost always seen. For anybody who enjoys birdlife, this is an opportunity to see such species as the anhinga, wood ibis, pileated woodpecker, and prothonotary warbler.

For generations, the Alapaha River in Georgia has scarcely been known by any sportsmen except fishermen in the vicinity.

The river can also produce a good meal for the canoeist who likes to fish. Largemouth bass, bluegills, chain pickerel, and channel catfish await the angler. The area's hunting is widely known.

WILDERNESS CAMPING ON CANOE TRAILS IN THE OKEFENOKEE SWAMP

The Okefenokee National Wildlife Refuge has 13 designated canoe trips, which range in lengths from 12 miles (2 days) to 55 miles (6 days).

1. Each canoe trail is limited to one party daily, and each party is limited to a maximum of 10 canoes and 20 persons. Canoeists are responsible for keeping trails free of litter. Litter must be held and carried out of the swamp. Any litter left by previous parties should be retrieved. Motors are not permitted.

2. Each traveler is required by law to have a Coast-Guard approved life preserver in his possession. Each canoe must contain a compass and a flashlight. Each canoeist must register when entering and leaving the swamp. Because of danger from alligators, pets may not be taken into the swamp. For the same reason, swimming is not permitted. Minimum party size for safety is two persons. Parties will not be permitted to launch later than 10 a.m., to insure that the overnight stop is reached before dark.

3. Daytime temperatures are mostly mild. But during June, July, August, and September, the swamp can be hot and humid with air temperatures above 90°F. Winter days range from below 40°F. to 80°F., but much of the time temperatures are in the 50s and 60s. Summer nights are warm, and winter nighttime temperatures can be near or below freezing. Record lows

have dipped to 18°F. The rainy season is normally from June through September. Many summer afternoons are drenched with localized thundershowers. Lightning is probably the most dangerous feature of an Okefenokee experience.

4. The swamp terrain is flat; there is no fast water and very little dry land. Your paddle will be used every inch of the way as you wind through cypress forests or cross open "prairies" exposed to the sun and wind. You may have to get out of your canoe and push across peat blow-ups or shallow water. Water levels in the Okefenokee Swamp sometimes become too low to permit use of certain trails. When this occurs, parties holding reservations are notified.

5. Overnight camping is permitted only at designated overnight stops. You must register at each stop. Since firm land is not available at all overnight stops, a 20 X 28-foot wooden platform is provided. Pop tents are recommended. No nails should be used, and no trees or limbs should be cut. Open fires are not permitted except at specified areas, so stoves that use gasoline, bottled gas, or similar types of fuel will be required if you plan to cook meals. You must remain at the designated overnight area between sunset and sunrise. You may camp only one night at each rest stop. Portable toilets with disposable bags are required.

6. Wildlife abounds in the Okefenokee every month of the year. Sandhill cranes, ducks, and other migratory birds are most numerous from November through March. Otter are commonly seen during cold weather when alligators are relatively inactive. Alligators are active in the summer and are observed sunning on banks mostly during spring and fall.

7. Sport fishing is permitted during daylight hours in accordance with Georgia state law and refuge regula-

tions. Live minnows are not permitted as bait in Okefenokee waters. Bass fishing is best in early spring and late fall, but a lot depends upon water levels, moon phase, weather, and the skill of the fisherman.

8. Canoe trips into the Okefenokee wilderness may be arranged in advance or on a first-come basis. For permits and reservations, write or phone well in advance of planned trip to:

> Refuge Manager
> Okefenokee National Wildlife Refuge
> P.O. Box 117
> Waycross, Georgia 31501
> Phone: 912/283-2580

The following information should be submitted with your request for a permit.

1. Date trip is planned.
2. Choices of canoe trails.
3. Expected number of canoes in party (a maximum of 10 canoes—20 persons—is permitted).
4. Name of person in charge.
5. Names and addresses of all participants.

WILDERNESS WATERWAY OF THE EVERGLADES NATIONAL PARK

The Everglades National Park has established a 100-mile wilderness waterway on the west side of Florida, running from Everglades City to Flamingo. The waterway runs through creeks, rivers, and open bays in the mangrove wilderness of the park.

The waterway is for small craft only. Because of

On the west side of Florida, from Everglades City to Flamingo, runs a 100-mile wilderness waterway in Everglades National Park. Credit: Florida Department of Commerce.

overhanging brush and narrow creeks, it is not recommended for boats with cabins or high windshields or
boats over 18 feet long.

You need 2 days to run the waterway, round trip, by
outboard. You need 7 days to make the trip, one way,
by canoe. Some 17 campsites have been set up along the
waterway. Most sites have picnic tables, grills, and trash
receptacles. Some campsites have pit toilets. Rules
require that the campsite be clean.

Persons taking the trip should check in and out with a
park ranger at either entrance, giving him a float plan
that includes expected times for making the trip.

Wildlife is plentiful along the waterway. Birds include
bald eagles, swallow-tailed kites, herons, egrets, and
ospreys. Animals likely to be seen are black bears,
bobcats, and raccoons. Perhaps the most interesting
critters are the ever-present alligators. Sometimes rattlesnakes and cottonmouths are seen.

Saltwater fishing requires no fishing license, and the
fishing for mullet, redfish, snook, and tarpon is excellent.

Hunting and firearms are not permitted along the
waterway or in the park.

Mosquitoes, sand flies, and other annoying insects are
abundant in the park throughout the summer. Insect
repellents are a must during these months.

High humidity and pleasantly warm temperatures
characterize the climate of the Everglades. During the
summer, temperatures range in the 80s and 90s, and
you may get frequent torrential local downpours and
lightning storms.

Winters are normally pleasant and clear, but in an
occasional cold wave temperatures may drop to a low of
30°F.

Every year between June and November, some 8 to

10 tropical storms build up in the Atlantic or Gulf and spin their way up through the Caribbean. Some of these storms intensify to hurricane strength (winds above 74 miles per hour) and threaten the mainland. Some years, as many as two or three of these storms may strike the coast. In other years, they all may blow themselves out somewhere in the North Atlantic.

Anybody who launches a boat in Florida waters during the hurricane season should be aware of expected weather conditions. Boaters at all times should pay close attention to posted storm warnings.

17

Swamp-Camping Ethic

In many areas of our nation, swamps—both large and small—are the last of nature's wild areas. Partly because of their forbidding mystique and partly because of their stubborn resistance to saws and shovels, our remaining swamps stand as a symbol of the wildness that once covered this land.

Today our swamps serve as timber producers, water-storage areas, wildlife breeding grounds, hideaways for endangered plants and animals, and perhaps most important, a place where you can visit and feel that you've stepped back in time.

Few places of such mysterious adventure are available to the sportsmen of our modern age. In order to preserve the true wildness that is left in our remaining swamps, it is the duty of every swamp camper to adopt the swamp-camping ethic: that is, to *leave no trace of our brief visit.*

To accomplish this goal we must practice what, for the lack of a better name, we can call zero-impact camping. The ingredients of zero-impact camping are known, or should be known, by every sportsman. It seems redundant to repeat them. But on almost every trip into a swamp, I see the ugly reminders that someone didn't stop to think, or perhaps doesn't care, how he was destroying this precious piece of wild America bit by bit. I will give you the ingredients for zero-impact camping in hopes that on your trips you will help keep our swamps free of the scars of man.

1. Respect the rights of the swamp owner or authority. Get hunting, fishing, and/or camping permission before entering.

2. Be sure to bring out the litter you take in. Also bring out any litter of thoughtless visitors that you find. The practice of burying trash is not acceptable in the fragile swamp environment. Wild animals dig it up, and high water washes it up. If you brought something in, you should bring it out.

3. If you use an open fire, burn only dead wood. Always stay with your fire or make sure it is out. Many of our swamps are actually peat bogs. Peat can burn underground for many yards. Don't build your fire on peat. The best policy, if you have the least doubt, is to use a stove and forego the open fire. When striking camp, make sure your fire is out and destroy all signs of a fire ring and fire.

4. If you use a four-wheel-drive vehicle, trail bike, or all-terrain vehicle, disturb the ground as little as possible. Don't have a mud rally or try to cut figure eights. These scars can be damaging with permanent effects.

5. Treat all living trees as though they were untouchable. Do not drive nails, cut initials, or otherwise damage trees. Do not hang lanterns next to trees. Heat from the lantern kills the adjacent bark. Don't wrap

In order to preserve the wilderness of our swamps, we swamp campers must practice the swamp-camping ethic: leave no trace of our brief visit. Credit: Georgia Industry & Trade.

wire or rope around trees. When left attached, wire and rope will girdle trees.

6. Dispose of human waste properly as discussed elsewhere in this book. There is nothing more degrading than to find a campsite deep in a swamp that looks like a septic-tank spill.

7. Avoid spilling oil and gas. When using an outboard motor, be as careful as possible.

8. Respect and obey the game-and-fish laws of the swamp. They are for your future enjoyment and the future of our wildlife.

By following these common-sense rules, we will have zero-impact camping. No one will know we've been there. This approach, practiced by all sportsmen, will lead to a swamp-camping ethic that will assure all swamp visitors now and in the future a wild environment to enjoy.

18

Suppliers of Swamp-Camping Equipment

It is often difficult to find the equipment you need for swamp-camping expeditions, so I've compiled this list of sources for your convenience.

The equipment listed here and mentioned elsewhere in this book is gear that I know is practical and proven for swamp use. There are many other brands and suppliers whose equipment might work just as well or even better. I just haven't tested those others myself. Since swamp-camping equipment is so essential to your well-being, I believe I should stick to what I know best.

Jungle Hammock
P & S Sales
P.O. Box 45095
Tulsa, Oklahoma 74145

Tents
Coleman Co.
250 N. St. Francis
Wichita, Kansas 67201

Camel Tents
P.O. Box 835
Knoxville, Tennessee 37901

Sunshine Tarp Co.
P.O. Box 806
Chatsworth, California 91311

Sleeping Bags
Country Ways
3500 Hwy 101 S.
Minnetonka, Minnesota 55343

Camp 7
802 S. Sherman St.
Longmont, Colorado 80501

Mattress
Cascade Designs
568 First Avenue S.
Seattle, Washington 98104

Gander Mountain, Inc.
P.O. Box 248
Wilmot, Wisconsin 53192

Gas Lanterns
Coleman Co.
250 N. St. Francis
Wichita, Kansas 67201

World Famous Sales
3580 N. Elston Avenue
Chicago, Illinois 60618

Candle Lantern and Candles
Waters, Inc.
111 E. Sheridan St.
Ely, Minnesota 55731

Mallory Duracell Flashlight
Eastern Mountain Sports
1041 Commonwealth Avenue
Boston, Massachusetts 02215

Camp Stoves
Coleman Co.
250 N. St. Francis
Wichita, Kansas 67201

Kangaroo Products
815 Houser Way N.
Renton, Washington 98055

Trailblazer, Inc.
2971 S. Madison
Wichita, Kansas 67216

Cook Kits
Palco Products
P.O. Box 88
Slatersville, Rhode Island
02876

Mirro Aluminum Co.
P.O. Box 409
Manitowoc, Wisconsin 54220

Dutch Ovens
Lodge Manufacturing Co.
P.O. Box 380
S. Pittsburg, Tennessee 37380

Water Containers
Igloo Corp.
P.O. Box 19322
Houston, Texas 77024

Thermos-King Seeley
Thermos Avenue
Norwich, Connecticut 06360

Porta-Toilet
Laacke & Joys Co.
1433 N. Water St.
Milwaukee, Wisconsin 53202

Camouflage Clothing
Mason Athletic Co.
P.O. Box 1887
Gastonia, North Carolina 28052

Winter Clothing
Columbia Sportswear
P.O. Box 03239
Portland, Oregon 97203

Recreational Equipment, Inc.
1525 11th Avenue
Seattle, Washington 98122

Boots
L. L. Bean, Inc.
Freeport, Maine 04033

Royal Red Ball
58 Maple St.
Naugatuck, Connecticut 06770

Jungle Boots
P & S Sales
P.O. Box 45095
Tulsa, Oklahoma 74145

Bill's Military Stores
18 W. Duval
Jacksonville, Florida 32202

Knives
Schrade Cutlery Corp.
1776 Broadway
New York, New York 10019

Gutmann Co.
900 Columbus Avenue
Mount Vernon, New York
10550

Normark Corp.
1710 E. 78th Street
Minneapolis, Minnesota 55423

Precise–Leisure Div.–Esquire
3 Chestnut St.
Suffern, New York 10901

Machetes
P & S Sales
P.O. Box 45095
Tulsa, Oklahoma 74145

Waterproof Match Container
L. L. Bean, Inc.
Freeport, Maine 04033

Eastern Mountain Sports
1041 Commonwealth Avenue
Boston, Massachusetts 02215

Survival Gear
Survival Systems, Inc.
1830 S. Baker Avenue
Ontario, California 91761

Waterproof Bags
Phoenix Products, Inc.
U.S. Highway 421
Tyner, Kentucky 40486

Voyageurs Ltd.
P.O. Box 512-C
Shawnee Mission, Kansas 66201

Freeze-Dried Foods
Mountain House Div.
Oregon Freeze Dry Foods
P.O. Box 1048
Albany, Oregon 97321

Richmoor
P.O. Box 2728
Van Nuys, California 91404

Water-Purification Kit
American Water Purification,
Inc.
1990 Olivera Rd.
Concord, California 94520

Pirogues
Canoe and Trail Shop
624 Moss Street
New Orleans, Louisiana 70119

Canoes
Sportspal, Inc.
P.O. Box E
Tecumseh, Minnesota 49286

Sawyer Canoes
Box 452-C
Oscoda, Michigan 48750

Old Town Canoe Co.
Old Town, Maine 04468

Boats
Grumman Boats
Marathon, New York 13803

Small Outboard Motor
Mercury Marine
1939 Pioneer Road
Fond Du Lac, Wisconsin 54935

Personal Flotation Devices
Stearns Manufacturing Co.
Box 1498
St. Cloud, Minnesota 56301

**Backpack Fishing Rods and
Reels**
Daiwa Corp.
14011 S. Normandie Avenue
Gardena, California 90249

Eagle Claw
c/o Wright & McGill Co.
4245 East 46th Ave.
P.O. Box 16011
Denver, Colorado 80216

Backpacks
Diamond Brand Canvas
Products
Naples, North Carolina 28760

Camp Trails Co.
3920 W. Clarendon Avenue
Phoenix, Arizona 85019

Buck Lure
Buckstop Lure Co.
3015 Grow Road
Stanton, Michigan 48888

Compasses
Silva Co.
2466 State Rd. 39 N.
La Porte, Indiana 46350

Gutmann Co.
900 Columbus Avenue
Mount Vernon, New York
10550

Paddles
Nona
977 W. 19th St.
Costa Mesa, California 92627

Mohawk Paddle
P.O. Box 668
Longwood, Florida 32750

Mosquito Headnet
P & S Sales
P.O. Box 45095
Tulsa, Oklahoma 74145

Bowfishing Tackle
Cajun Archery Co.
Rt. 3, Box 88
New Iberia, Louisiana 70560

Index